# Agenda Worksheet

Meeting Date: _____

| Item | Purpose (Information, Review, Discuss, Decide) | Time Needed | Presenter/ Facilitator | Equipment/ Materials Needed |
|------|------------------------------------------------|-------------|------------------------|------------------------------|
|      |                                                |             |                        |                              |
|      |                                                |             |                        |                              |
|      |                                                |             |                        |                              |
|      |                                                |             |                        |                              |
|      |                                                |             |                        |                              |

THE JOSSEY-BASS ACADEMIC ADMINISTRATOR'S GUIDE TO

# Meetings

The Jossey-Bass Academic Administrator's Guides are designed to help new and experienced campus professionals when a promotion or move brings on new responsibilities, new tasks, and new situations. Each book focuses on a single topic, exploring its application to the higher education setting. These real-world guides provide advice about day-to-day responsibilities as well as an orientation to the organizational environment of campus administration. From department chairs to office staff supervisors, these concise resources will help college and university administrators understand and overcome obstacles to success.

We hope you will find this volume useful in your work. To that end, we welcome your reaction to this volume and to the series in general, including suggestions for future topics.

THE JOSSEY-BASS

# ACADEMIC ADMINISTRATOR'S GUIDE TO

# Meetings

## JANIS FISHER CHAN

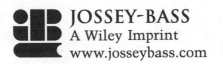

JOSSEY-BASS
A Wiley Imprint
www.josseybass.com

Published by Jossey-Bass
A Wiley Imprint
989 Market Street, San Francisco, CA 94103-1741   www.josseybass.com

Jossey-Bass books and products are available through most bookstores. To contact Jossey-Bass directly call our Customer Care Department within the U.S. at 800-956-7739, outside the U.S. at 317-572-3986 or fax 317-572-4002.

Jossey-Bass also publishes its books in a variety of electronic formats. Some content that appears in print may not be available in electronic books.

Library of Congress Cataloging-in-Publication Data

Chan, Janis Fisher.
    The Jossey-Bass academic administrator's guide to meetings / Janis Fisher Chan.—1st ed.
        p. cm.
Includes bibliographical references (p.      ) and index.
    ISBN 0-7879-6432-8 (alk. paper)
    1. College administrators—Handbooks, manuals, etc.   2. Meetings—Handbooks, manuals, etc.   3. Group facilitation—Handbooks, manuals, etc.   I. Title.
    LB2341 .C476 2003
    658.4'56—dc21

                                                                        2002153515

Printed in the United States of America
FIRST EDITION
*PB Printing*   10  9  8  7  6  5  4  3  2  1

# CONTENTS

**A**NYONE WHO WORKS in higher education understands that meetings are necessary—and sometimes a necessary evil. Meetings are the way that much of the business of the institution and the various groups it includes gets done. A successful meeting is one in which specific objectives are accomplished as efficiently as possible, and although participants might prefer to be doing something else, most will agree that the meeting was necessary and a good use of their time. An unsuccessful meeting, on the other hand, can result in poorly made decisions, unfinished business, and bad feelings all around.

As anyone who has ever tried it knows, running effective meetings in an academic setting presents some unique challenges. The wide range of people's schedules can make it difficult even to find a time to meet. Many people are so busy that it's asking a lot to expect them to make time for a meeting. And the very qualities that make academics so good at what they do—critical minds, the ability to think independently—can make it hard for them to work well in groups.

This book will help you address these challenges. It provides practical information and guidelines that you can use immediately to make sure that your meetings run more smoothly and efficiently, are more productive, and make the best use of your group members' valuable time. Although the ideas and suggestions in these pages are applicable to any meeting, we focus on the small and midsize meetings that are held to accomplish the business of the institution: regular and periodic department, interdepartment, administrative, and staff meetings; committee meetings; task force meetings; and nonrecurring meetings held for a special purpose. We will not directly address the special needs of other types of meetings, such as conferences, university-wide faculty meetings, and professional development workshops.

## WHO SHOULD READ THIS BOOK

You'll find this book useful if you are an administrator, faculty member, or graduate student who sometimes takes on the responsibility for convening or conducting a meeting or if you are someone who might need to do so in the future. You'll find it essential if you are a new academic or administrative manager, supervisor, team leader, or committee chair with limited experience in running meetings. Even if you have been leading meetings for many years, you might well find that the book gives you new ideas and perspectives that can help you make your already good meetings even better.

## WHAT'S IN THE BOOK?

The following is an overview of what you'll find in these pages. Chapter One presents an overview of the reasons for holding meetings, factors that determine whether a meeting needs to be held, and the criteria that a meeting must meet to be successful. Chapter Two examines who does what to plan, prepare for, conduct, and follow up a meeting. In Chapter Three you'll find a step-by-step process, including checklists and a worksheet, for planning a successful meeting. Guidelines for facilitating productive meetings, including how to open and close a meeting, keep the group on track, and manage the group dynamics are covered in Chapter Four. Finally, Chapter Five offers guidelines for making decisions in meetings, including when and how to use consensus.

# ABOUT THE AUTHOR

JANIS FISHER CHAN, a writer, editor, trainer, and instructional designer for more than twenty years, specializes in helping people communicate clearly. As co-owner of a successful training company, she developed and conducted customized workshops on topics that included meeting planning, business writing, interpersonal communication, performance management, and making presentations. In addition to conducting workshops, she now provides freelance services as an instructional designer, writer, and editor. She is coauthor of several business writing books, including *Professional Writing Skills, Grammar for Grownups, Writing Performance Documentation, How to Write Reports and Proposals,* and *Just Commas,* all available through www.writeitwell.com, and the author of three self-study courses for the American Management Association: *Successful Business Communications, Managing Your Priorities,* and *Making Successful Presentations.* Her e-mail address is janisdee@attbi.com.

THE JOSSEY-BASS ACADEMIC ADMINISTRATOR'S GUIDE TO

# Meetings

# What Makes a Meeting Work?

N OT ANOTHER ONE OF THOSE $&*! MEETINGS!"

Jennifer and Tyrone, both biology professors, are fed up with their weekly department meeting. "We never get anything done," Jennifer complains as she and Tyrone head across campus to the parking lot. "As far as I'm concerned, it's a waste of two perfectly good hours."

"Especially when we run over, like today, when Phil and Arlene got into that stupid argument," Tyrone says. "I've had enough. I'm skipping next week's meeting—I'm behind on my research project as it is. It won't make any difference—no one will even notice I'm not there."

Unfortunately, Tyrone was right. His absence made no difference to the next meeting, which was primarily a series of announcements, followed by a continuation of the discussion between Phil and Arlene, who had been disagreeing for some time about an issue of interest mostly to themselves. "I can't understand why the chair lets them go on and on like that," Jennifer said when she filled Tyrone in on the meeting he had missed. "But I was smart this time. I sat in the back of the room so I could review the notes for my journal article. At least I got *something* done."

## INTRODUCTION

Like most people who work in higher education, Jennifer and Tyrone are always busy, with many competing demands on their time. Their conversation makes it clear that the weekly department meeting is a demand that they would prefer to ignore.

Their complaints indicate that the biology department chair needs to think about why she holds a faculty meeting every week and what she could do to make the meeting useful to everyone who attends. She needs to consider the many good reasons to hold a meeting, as well as the many times when a meeting may not be the best way to accomplish her purpose. She also needs to think about the criteria a meeting must meet if it is to make good use of the participants' valuable time.

## REASONS FOR MEETINGS

On any given day, there is likely to be a wide range of meetings taking place on any campus: regular weekly, biweekly, and monthly department, interdepartment, staff, and committee meetings; meetings called for a special purpose such as to make an emergency decision; occasional meetings of a task force or a group that is working on a project. Meetings are the way much of the important work of any institution is accomplished.

Not all communication requires face-to-face interaction, of course. But bringing people together for a meeting is useful when they need to:

- Share information

- Share ideas, perspectives, and experience

- Identify and resolve problems

- Do planning

- Discuss issues and make decisions

- Build community

- Clear the air

Most meetings have more than one purpose. Imagine that you are sitting in on a monthly department meeting. You might notice that the group begins with several informational items, including the change in the deadline for a grant application. Next, they hear a report about an upcoming conference. After that, they discuss whether to add a new course to next year's curriculum. Finally, they do the preliminary planning for a graduation event.

To understand what makes a meeting work, however, it is helpful to look at the most common purposes one at a time.

## Sharing Information

A well-run meeting can be an efficient way to pass on information: someone from information technology makes a presentation on database changes; a human resources specialist explains new health plan options; committee members report their progress on specific projects; a department manager or chair discusses a change in policy that has come down from administration. All meetings have an informative component, and for some meetings, the sharing of information is the primary purpose.

What's important to consider is that not all information needs to be shared in a meeting. Simple announcements can usually be made more efficiently by sending out a memo or e-mail message. Meetings are useful for passing on information when people need to be able to ask questions, voice concerns, or make suggestions. For instance, a change in the summer schedule for the library could most efficiently be announced in an e-mail message, while substantial changes in an administrative procedure might be best explained in a meeting.

## Sharing Ideas, Perspectives, and Experience

On a campus, where many people work independently, meetings are among the few occasions when people within a department or across departments come together. Thus, meetings offer unique opportunities for people to share what they know with others and to learn from one another. The experience of long-time faculty or staff members can be invaluable to newer members of a department. Similarly, the ideas that younger people bring to the table can help everyone see old issues in a new way. In well-run meetings, the facilitator helps the various ideas, perspectives, and experience emerge by encouraging participation, respect for different points of view, open discussion, and active listening.

## Identifying and Resolving Problems

Problem solving is one of the key reasons for holding meetings. The diversity of perspectives and knowledge within a group increases the chances of coming up with good solutions. By bouncing ideas off one another, people are likely to come up with more, and better, ideas than they might come up with if they were pondering the problem on their own.

Not everyone in the room needs to be directly affected by the problem for the problem-solving process to work, although at least one person in the group needs to "own" the problem. The process works best when the facilitator helps the participants articulate an objective that clearly states what the situation will be when the problem has been solved—"When we have solved this problem, we will have a written procedure to follow that ensures we meet our administrative deadlines." It also works best when the group comes up with a detailed action plan that states who will do what to carry out the solution.

## Planning

A common reason to hold meetings is to plan something, such as a conference, a program, a reorganization, or the implementation of new procedures. The group works together to identify what needs to be done, establish a timetable, and determine who will do what to accomplish the objective. Planning meetings are most successful when everyone involved has a stake in the outcome—in other words, when the people at the meeting are somehow concerned that what is being planned comes off well. Successful planning meetings also include people who have knowledge or expertise that is essential to the planning process. A group that is planning a conference, for example, might need the help of someone who is experienced in planning such events, because that individual knows what must be considered to put on a successful conference.

Not all the work involved in planning has to be accomplished at the first meeting. One common objective of a planning meeting is to identify what needs to be done and make specific assignments for individuals or small groups to carry out.

## Discussing Issues and Making Decisions

Meetings are opportunities for people to make decisions—sometimes, very important decisions—about issues that affect them and others. Again, the diversity of viewpoints, knowledge, expertise, and experience can help the group make better decisions than an individual might make alone. Also, participation in the decision-making process itself can be crucial if people are to understand, accept, and support the decision that is made.

Good decision-making is a difficult business. The facilitator must thoroughly understand the different ways that groups can make decisions and be able to guide participants through the process. Because this process is so complex, we have provided detailed guidelines in Chapters Four and Five.

## Clearing the Air

As mentioned earlier, most meetings have more than one purpose. There is one kind of meeting, however, that should never be held in conjunction with another meeting. "Clear-the-air" meetings are intended to address frustrations and tensions that have built up over a single issue or within the group over time. A clear-the-air meeting might be needed if some members of a group are upset about a decision and refuse to carry it out, if they snipe at one another or refuse to participate during meetings, or if they have made it known that they feel unhappy with the "way things are done around here."

A clear-the-air meeting should have only one purpose: to provide a safe, neutral environment in which people can voice their feelings, concerns, and grievances. The objective is not to resolve the issues that surface. The issues should simply be voiced, clarified, and recorded. One or more separate meetings should then be scheduled to address them.

Clear-the-air meetings are for situations that affect everyone, not just two or three individuals. They require very careful facilitation. The facilitator must know how to handle emotional outbursts, keep the meeting from degenerating into a complaint session, encourage active listening, and so on. In Chapter Four, you'll find more detailed information on handling difficult situations.

## Building Community

Although we've listed community building separately, it does not really stand alone as a purpose for a meeting. Every successful meeting helps a group build a sense of community, which is especially important in academic institutions where people do not always work with their colleagues on a day-to-day basis. The process of working together toward shared goals helps people get to know one another and provides a foundation that makes it easier for the group to deal with the difficult issues that are bound to come up from time to time.

It's important not to call a meeting solely to build community. People dislike being called to a meeting that has no clear purpose. When the only purpose is to give people a chance to mingle, it's better to hold a dinner party or a picnic. But when a meeting called to accomplish specific business goes well, and people leave feeling that the meeting was productive, community building happens.

# WHEN A MEETING IS NOT NEEDED

Just as there are many good reasons for holding meetings, there are times when meetings should not be held. Some of them are described below.

## Information Can Be Relayed Through Other Means

When the primary purpose for holding a meeting is to pass on information, consider whether a meeting is really needed. The key question is this: Will people need to ask questions, voice concerns, or make suggestions after they receive the information? If not, it's probably a waste of everyone's time to hold a meeting just to present information that could be passed on more efficiently in a memo or an e-mail, or by telephone.

Even when you determine that an informational meeting does make sense, consider giving participants the details in written form ahead of time. That way, the meeting itself can be used for the activities that require face-to-face interaction, such as asking and responding to questions.

## Key People Cannot Be Present

There are few things more frustrating than making time for a meeting only to find that the work of the meeting cannot be accomplished because a key person is not there. Make sure you know who needs to be there to accomplish the objectives of the meeting. If key people can't be available at the time you plan to hold the meeting, reschedule. Similarly, if an essential person has to cancel, even at the last minute, consider canceling the meeting unless there is something else worthwhile to do with the time. See Chapter Three for more details about making sure the right people attend your meetings.

### You Only Want the Group to Rubber-Stamp a Decision

There is a big difference between making a decision and agreeing with one that has already been made. People dislike being asked to attend a meeting where all they are expected to do is say, "Sure, go ahead, that's okay with me." If the decision has already been made, hold a meeting only if you sincerely want the group's feedback and are willing to reconsider, or if you think it is important to explain your reasons for the decision. Otherwise, use a memo or e-mail message to communicate the decision to the group. For a detailed discussion of the decision-making process, see Chapter Five.

### People Are Distracted by Other Priorities

Unless there is a crucial issue that needs to be addressed immediately, avoid holding meetings at times when people are likely to be concerned with or overwhelmed by other priorities. For example, try not to hold meetings during the first and last weeks of a term, on the day before a holiday, or during midterm or finals weeks. For faculty, summer and holiday breaks are usually poor times for meetings, while for staff, those times can be good for meetings because the campus is quieter.

## CRITERIA FOR AN EFFECTIVE MEETING

Everyone who has ever attended a meeting knows the difference between a meeting that works and one that doesn't. Think about meetings you've attended. Which ones were successful? Why? Which didn't work? What went wrong?

When people are asked to identify the factors that make a meeting successful, they mention the same points again and again—probably some of the same points you would raise yourself. The points forming the criteria for a successful meeting are briefly discussed below. In later chapters, you will see how these criteria serve as the basis for actions you can take to improve the meetings you conduct.

*The meeting is necessary, has a clear purpose and objective, and addresses relevant, important topics.* It's easier for people to focus on the issues and stay on track when they know that the meeting is important and what it is expected to accomplish. If a meeting has no clear purpose, don't be surprised if they wonder aloud why in the world they bothered to come. Chapter Three presents a step-by-step planning process that helps you determine whether the meeting is necessary, identify the purpose and objectives, and decide what topics to address.

*The agenda can be covered in the time available.* Too many items to address in too little time is a recipe for failure. Decisions will be made hastily or not at all, and it will be difficult to end the meeting on time without dropping items for which people have carefully prepared. Be realistic about the time you have available. If there are enough topics for a two-hour meeting but you only have an hour and a half, save some of the topics for another meeting. The planning process in Chapter Three also walks you through the process of developing a realistic agenda.

*Roles and responsibilities are clear.* In a successful meeting, all the people involved know what they are expected to do. Without such clarity, meetings often become disorganized and fail to achieve even the simplest objectives. Chapter Two provides a detailed discussion of the roles and responsibilities of the convener, the facilitator, the recorder, the presenters—and the participants.

*The key people are present and everyone comes prepared.* As mentioned earlier, there is little point holding a meeting if key people cannot be there—the work simply cannot get done. There is also little point to meeting when people are not prepared to make their presentations or discuss the issues. Unable to accomplish the objectives, participants generally leave such meetings frustrated and grumbling. As you will see in Chapter Three, your questions when planning a meeting should include, "Who needs to be there?" and "What do people need to do before the meeting?"

*The meeting starts and ends on time.* Nearly everyone who is asked to describe a successful meeting says that it starts when it is scheduled to start and ends when it is scheduled to end. Thus, after determining what to include on the agenda, you need to determine how much time each item will take—then, if you don't have enough time to cover everything, you must decide what can be dropped. During the meeting, you need to monitor the proceedings to ensure that the individual items start and stop on time. In Chapters Three and Four, you'll find detailed guidelines that will help you set up a timetable and stick to it.

*The meeting is held at a convenient time and in a comfortable, private place.* The timing and physical environment can have a significant impact on the success of a meeting. For example, early morning meetings can be difficult for some participants, and noisy rooms make it hard to hear. The time and effort expended to make people as comfortable as possible pays off in terms of increased enthusiasm, attention, and participation. Chapter Three presents a discussion of factors to consider about time and place that affect meeting success.

*Everyone participates, and people respect and are considerate of one another.* Although there are different ways in which people can participate—for example, not everyone needs to talk all the time—it is important that everyone in the room *be* in the room. If people's bodies are present but their minds are elsewhere, there is little reason for a meeting. A successful meeting is one in which people pay attention and make relevant, useful contributions while showing consideration for one another even when their views on the topics differ. In Chapter Four, you'll find facilitation strategies for increasing participation and improving group dynamics.

*The meeting stays on track.* Hard on the heels of "start and end on time" as a factor in meeting success is the ability of the facilitator to manage discussions so that the meeting stays on track. That's not always easy, but you'll find suggestions for how to keep a meeting focused on the agenda items in Chapter Four.

*People are clear about the disposition of agenda items, action plans are developed, and action plans are followed up.* When describing successful meetings, people often mention the need for clarity and closure. They want to leave knowing what they have accomplished and what happens next. They also want to be sure that the actions they have decided on are actually carried out, which means that someone must take responsibility for following up and reporting back to the group. See Chapters Four and Five for detailed information about ways to close meetings and how to do action planning.

## WHAT'S NEXT

In this chapter you have examined the reasons for holding meetings and reasons why meetings are not always needed, as well as the key factors that make meetings work. In the next chapter, you will find a detailed discussion of the roles and responsibilities of the people involved in convening, running, and participating in a meeting.

# 2

# Roles and Responsibilities

ISN'T ANYONE WRITING THIS STUFF DOWN?"

The Student Services biweekly staff meeting was going well. The group had discussed several important items and made key decisions about how to implement recent administrative policy changes. During the discussion, people had raised a number of issues that would need to be addressed at the next meeting.

Ten minutes before the meeting was scheduled to end, Laura asked Ted, who was facilitating, "Before we leave, can we take a few minutes to review the decisions we've made and the issues we've brought up today?"

"Good idea," Ted said. There was a long pause. "Let's see. I think we decided to change the procedure for scheduling Student Center activities. Right? And didn't someone volunteer to clarify what the president meant in last Thursday's memo?" Ted looked around the group. "What else?"

Sylvia spoke up. "I wanted to make sure that we talked about the staff assignments next time."

"Right," Ted said. There was another long period of silence.

"But what changes did we actually agree on for the scheduling procedures?" Laura asked. After listening to a few mumbled responses, she said, unable to keep the tone of frustration out of her voice, "We spent twenty minutes making that decision. Wasn't someone taking notes?" It turned out that no one was, and now it was too late. The meeting was over, and another group was waiting impatiently in the hall outside the conference room.

# INTRODUCTION

Ted runs a good meeting. He knows how to manage a discussion and guide the group toward a decision. But he made one serious mistake: he forgot about the importance of making sure that someone was recording the group's issues, concerns, key discussion points, and decisions. Everyone assumed that someone was taking notes (doesn't someone usually take notes at meetings?), so no one bothered to write anything down, and much of the work done at the meeting was lost. Even if Ted were to try reconstructing what had taken place, his attention had been on keeping the meeting going smoothly, so he would find it difficult to remember everything.

A good meeting is, in some ways, like a stage production. It works well when all the roles and responsibilities are clear, when everyone knows what he or she is expected to do—and does it. In this chapter, we will look at the roles and responsibilities of the people involved in a meeting and why they are all important for a meeting to achieve its objectives.

# WHO DOES WHAT

For most meetings, there are five key roles that need to be filled:

*Convener:* The person who decides that a meeting needs to be held, identifies the topics that need to be addressed, and determines who needs to attend

*Facilitator:* The person who runs the meeting

*Presenters:* People who deliver information during the meeting

*Recorder:* The person who writes down key discussion points, ideas, and decisions

*Participants:* People who are invited to attend and participate in the meeting

*Support staff:* People who do the many tasks needed to make a meeting happen and run smoothly, such as administrative assistants and technical specialists

In many meetings, of course, people play more than one role. Just as the producer of a stage production might also direct the show or take one of the parts, the convener might also facilitate the meeting or present information. Just as the person in charge of the scripts might be one of the performers, the recorder can also be a participant. Meeting participants listen to others present information and also deliver information themselves.

What's important is that each role be filled and that people be clear about which role they are playing at a given time. In the role of performer, a producer needs to forget about keeping the show within budget and concentrate on her performance. Similarly, a facilitator can't focus on group dynamics while making a presentation.

Below are descriptions of the responsibilities that are specific to each of the key roles.

## Convener's Responsibilities

The convener is the person who calls the meeting. The convener might be the chair of a committee or task force, the head of a department, or a staff member who thinks there is a good reason to bring people together to discuss an issue.

But it's not enough simply to call a meeting. Like the producer of a stage production, who must decide what production to put on, select a director and a cast, choose the dates and the venue, find the funding, and so on, the convener must carry out several responsibilities that are crucial to a successful meeting. Those responsibilities include:

- Identifying the purpose and goals and developing the agenda

- Scheduling the meeting

- Deciding who should attend and notifying participants

- Making sure participants have the information they need ahead of time and know what to bring to the meeting

- When appropriate, scheduling outside presenters and making sure they know what's expected of them

- If necessary, selecting a facilitator and working with that person to plan and prepare for the meeting

- Following up to make sure that meeting results are communicated to participants and other appropriate individuals, and that action items are handled

Conveners often facilitate the meetings they call, but not always. Sometimes it's better to ask a member of the group to facilitate for all or part of a meeting, or to bring in an outside facilitator. For example:

- It's difficult to be a participant and a facilitator at the same time. If a convener wants to participate actively in a discussion, it's a good idea to ask someone else to facilitate, at least for that part of the meeting.

- Participants' perceptions that the convener has higher status and authority can keep them from speaking openly, especially if they disagree with the convener. In such situations, an outside facilitator can help to create a nonthreatening environment in which people feel more comfortable expressing their views.

- Conveners who lack confidence in their ability to do a good job of leading a meeting often prefer to hand over the facilitation responsibilities to someone who has good facilitation skills.

## Facilitator's Responsibilities

Even a stage production with one or two performers needs a director, an objective eye to guide the performers toward their goal. In the same way, every meeting, even one called on the spur of the moment with only a few participants, needs some level of facilitation, someone who keeps an eye on the time and the agenda and keeps the group moving towards its goals. While the group might be able to handle its own facilitation naturally for small, impromptu meetings, most meetings need a designated facilitator.

The facilitator's job is to conduct the meeting. To do that job, she must remain neutral and observant, focusing her attention on process and not taking sides in the discussions. A good facilitator encourages participants to share ideas and opinions, recognizes when a discussion has run its course, and provides the summaries and clarifications that ensure understanding. Sometimes she does little more than open the meeting, introduce the agenda items in order, and close the meeting. But sometimes she must direct the meeting as carefully as a director guides a stage production or a conductor leads an orchestra.

Whether the facilitator is the convener, a group member, or someone from outside the group, here are some of the functions that she needs to carry out:

- Work with the convener to clarify the meeting's expectations, purpose, and goals and perhaps to prepare the agenda
- Prepare presentations, materials, and activities
- Arrange for, supervise, and coordinate the room setup, including seating arrangements, audiovisual equipment and refreshments, if any, and arrive early enough to ensure that everything is ready
- Make sure the meeting sticks to the agenda and the timetable
- Open the meeting in a way that focuses people's attention and prepares them to handle the business of the meeting
- Manage discussions to encourage participation, keep the group focused, and ensure that no single individual or group dominates
- Summarize and clarify as needed to help everyone follow what's being said
- Manage the decision-making process
- Introduce presenters and make sure they stay within their designated times
- Handle difficult or unexpected situations if they arise
- Close the meeting in a way that ensures people know what took place, what was decided, who will do what, and what happens next
- If appropriate, conduct an evaluation of the meeting

*Note:* Facilitation is so important to a successful meeting that it is covered in its own chapter, Chapter Four.

## Presenters' Responsibilities

Many meetings include informal and/or formal presentations, the purpose of which is to provide participants with information about a specific topic. Presentations might be the most important part of a meeting, a small segment of the agenda, or the prelude to a decision-making or problem-solving process. In a successful meeting, each presentation provides relevant information in a way that helps participants understand it.

The presenters are often members of the group. For example, members of a task force might report the results of their research into the causes of a problem, or a faculty member might make a presentation about a new course he would like added to the curriculum.

Presenters can also come from outside the group. Someone from Library Services might attend a faculty meeting to explain new services that will be available next semester, or a group from another department might present information about their upcoming conference.

Whether presenters come from within or outside the group, they have certain responsibilities:

- *Come on time.* This is especially important for outside presenters, who might not need to be there for the whole meeting, but it's also important for participants whose presentations are on the agenda. Late presenters can quickly throw a meeting off track.

- *Be prepared.* A useful presentation includes the right information for the audience, presented in a way that the audience can easily

### USING A TIMEKEEPER AND A DOORKEEPER

To keep a meeting running smoothly, a facilitator must focus on process, time, and group dynamics all at once. That's hard to do. To help the facilitator out, groups sometimes use timekeepers and doorkeepers, roles that can be rotated among the participants or filled by support staff. The timekeeper watches the clock and lets the facilitator know if an agenda item needs to be wrapped up. The doorkeeper minimizes disruption by helping latecomers get seated and filling them in on what they have missed.

understand. Unplanned, sloppy presentations waste every-one's time.

- *Encourage questions.* Some presenters forget that a primary purpose of presenting information in a meeting is to allow people to comment, ask for clarification, or ask for additional information. Otherwise, the information could be provided more efficiently in another way.

- *Stay within their allotted time.* A common reason that meetings go overtime is that presentations go overtime. Presenters should be clearly told how much time they will have—including time for questions—and plan to include only the amount of information that can be delivered effectively in that amount of time.

- *Provide participants with relevant materials before the meeting.* Presenters should not ask people to use valuable meeting time to read things they could—and should—have read ahead of time. For example, if the presentation is a proposal for a new course, participants should receive the course description in time to read it before the meeting.

## Recorder's Responsibilities

In the scenario that began this chapter, valuable information was lost because no one was taking notes. The recorder is an often overlooked yet very important part of any successful meeting.

The recorder's responsibilities are deceptively simple: to capture the participants' key ideas, points, concerns, and decisions, and to capture them accurately. To do that job, the recorder must:

- Pay attention and listen closely

- Focus on what's important

- Ask questions as needed to clarify what people say

- Keep accurate notes, including a list of participants

- After the meeting, prepare and distribute a summary of the proceedings

## THE ROTATING RECORDER

In some groups, the same participant acts as recorder at every meeting, and this approach can cause problems:

- The recorder's responsibilities keep the person from fully participating in the meeting.
- If the person records by quietly taking notes, other participants may perceive him as a lesser member of the group, not a full participant.
- If the recorder uses an "open" recording method, standing at a flip chart in front of the group, he can be perceived as the group's leader.

To avoid these problems, rotate the recorder's role. At the end of each meeting, decide who will serve as recorder for the next; for longer meetings, pass the role to a new person every hour or so, or with every new agenda item.

The recorder can be one of the participants, support staff, or someone from outside brought in solely for the purpose of recording the proceedings. In groups that meet regularly, the role of recorder is often rotated among participants, or the recorder's role is filled by someone from the support staff who does not need to participate actively in the meeting. For meetings held with the primary purpose of discussing difficult or sensitive issues or making complex decisions, it can be helpful to use an outside recorder who is neutral on the issues and can focus on accurately capturing the proceedings, leaving all the group members free to keep their attention on the issues and participate actively in the discussions.

There are two primary methods for recording the proceedings of a meeting: the recorder sits among the participants or off to the side and takes notes, or the recorder stands in front of the group near the facilitator and writes on flip chart pages that everyone can see.

The more "open" method of recording, which allows the group to see what the recorder is writing down, has some obvious advantages, including the following:

- Participants stay more connected to what's going on because the key points from discussions are always right in front of them.

- Participants can immediately correct inaccuracies or omissions in the written record.

- The recorder can post the flip chart pages generated during a discussion so the facilitator can use them to summarize when the group is ready to make a decision.

- Participants can see that their comments, ideas, concerns, and so on, have been captured.

"Open" recording is most useful when the group is brainstorming ideas, generating solutions to a problem, discussing issues, or commenting on a proposal. For "ordinary" business meetings, where the agenda consists mostly of information sharing and short presentations, quiet note taking, which can be done efficiently on a laptop computer, is usually sufficient.

Chapter Four provides more suggestions for recording meeting proceedings.

## Participants' Responsibilities

Meetings don't happen without participants—and sometimes not much happens even when the room is filled. For a meeting to achieve its goals, the participants must do what their title implies: *participate*. The best planning and the most skilled facilitator can't do much to make a meeting work unless the people who are attending actively involve themselves.

To respect the value of their colleagues' time, participants must:

- *Come on time.* One of the primary complaints people have about meetings is that they never start on time. Yet the same people often make little effort to be in the room and ready to go when the meeting is scheduled to begin.

- *Be prepared.* It's frustrating to everyone when a few people have not done their "homework"—for example, when people have not read materials that were handed out in advance and thus are not prepared to discuss them.

- *Participate actively.* Active participation does not mean that people have to talk all the time. But it does mean paying attention and speaking up when it's appropriate.

- *Share ideas and perspectives.* One of the great benefits of bringing people together for a meeting is the opportunity to hear other people's ideas and points of view, so it is important that participants be willing to share them.

- *Listen to and respect other participants.* Listening actively is a skill that some people find difficult to master, especially when the speaker is expressing a view that differs from their own. For the give and take of a successful meeting, however, it is essential that participants really listen to one another, and that they respect differing points of view.

- *Ask for clarification as needed.* A good facilitator will try to clarify as needed to ensure that people understand what's being said. But the facilitator doesn't always know when someone has not understood something, and participants must be willing to speak up if something is unclear.

- *Speak up if the meeting seems to be off track.* If the facilitator seems unwilling or unable to keep the meeting on track, participants should be willing to point out that people seem to have departed from the agenda.

- *Avoid side discussions, distracting activities, and obstructive behavior.* Just as a professor expects students to behave appropriately in a classroom, meeting participants are responsible for behaving appropriately in a meeting. Such activities as whispering to a neighbor, tapping on the table, making inappropriate comments, grading papers, reading e-mails, telling jokes, or challenging everything that's said make everyone uncomfortable and make it difficult, if not impossible, for the meeting to accomplish its goals.

It is not unusual for people to play different roles within the same meeting. The facilitator and the recorder might also be participants, commenting on the issues and joining in the decisions. Different people might facilitate different agenda items.

What's important is that all the people in the room be clear about which role they—and the others—are playing at a given time. One way to emphasize that someone is changing roles is to say, "Okay, I'm taking off the facilitator's hat now so I can comment on what Jillian just said," or "I'm handing the recorder's hat to Phil for the next agenda item so I can participate in the discussion." You don't have to use real hats, of course—but you could!

## Support Staff Responsibilities

It takes a lot of work to make a meeting happen, and even more to make it a success. Good support staff—office managers, administrative assistants, technical experts—can be very helpful. Part of the planning process should be deciding what tasks and responsibilities can be carried out by support staff—preparing and distributing agendas, sending out notifications and reminders, arranging for and setting up the room, developing overhead transparencies or PowerPoint slides, and so forth.

# WHAT'S NEXT

In this chapter, you have reviewed the roles and responsibilities of the people involved in a meeting. In the next chapter, you will find a step-by-step process for planning a meeting so that it achieves specific objectives as efficiently and effectively as possible.

# 3

# The Meeting Planning Process

W HAT WENT WRONG?"

Marla, a new associate dean of student affairs, received an e-mail from Facilities informing her that she and her staff will be moved to temporary offices next month while their building is being renovated. The e-mail included the date of the move and the location of the temporary offices, which are on the ground floor of a building on the other side of campus.

Immediately after reading the e-mail, Marla dropped a quick note to her staff, asking them to meet with her in the conference room at 4:30 that afternoon. The meeting, which Marla had expected to run for only a few minutes, kept going until after 5:30 and accomplished very little. Only six of the eleven staff members showed up, because several already had other commitments. Instead of discussing what had to be done to prepare for the move, which was what Marla had intended, the group kept asking questions—"Why do we have to move so far away?" "How long will we be in the temporary office?" "Do they expect us to pack up the computers?"—that Marla couldn't answer. As the meeting finally broke up, Marla heard one staff member grumble, "*That* was a waste of time, and now I'm going to miss my ride."

## INTRODUCTION

Meetings can be extremely useful vehicles for getting things done. Unfortunately, too many meetings end like Marla's, with people grumbling that the meeting was a waste of time.

Marla made several common mistakes when she decided on the spur of the moment to call a meeting. For example, she did not decide exactly what she wanted the meeting to accomplish, she didn't provide information ahead of time so people could come prepared, and she didn't think about what her staff needed to know about the move. She also did not stop to think about who needed to be there or consider people's schedules when she chose the meeting time.

This kind of unplanned meeting nearly always falls short of expectations. Without a clear purpose, people spend a lot of time figuring out what the meeting is supposed to be about. Without the right people there, it can be difficult or impossible to get anything done. If the time is inconvenient, participants might find it hard to focus on the matter at hand.

The key to a successful meeting is careful, thoughtful planning. In this chapter you will find details about how to plan meetings that are, unlike Marla's, useful and productive.

# THE MEETING PLANNING PROCESS

How long it takes to plan a meeting depends on the type of meeting, the number and complexity of the issues, and other factors. But for a meeting to be successful, the planning process should include the following:

- *Identifying the purpose and objective.* Why are you calling the meeting? What do you expect to accomplish? What will the "product" from the meeting look like?

- *Drawing up a preliminary list of agenda items.* What information will be given to participants at the meeting? What topics and issues will participants discuss? What decisions do participants need to make?

- *Deciding how long the meeting will be.* How long will it take to cover each agenda item? How much time is available for the meeting? Will there be enough time to cover everything?

- *Deciding whom to invite.* Who must be there for the meeting to achieve its objectives? Who else should also be invited?

- *Choosing the time and place.* Considering people's schedules, what's the most convenient time? Of the places available, which is the most convenient, comfortable, and private?

- *Choosing a facilitator and recorder.* Will you facilitate the meeting yourself? Will one or more of the participants serve as facilitator? Who will serve as recorder?

- *Preparing the agenda.* What's the best sequence for the items? How much time should be allocated to each item? Who will present or facilitate each item?

- *Notifying participants.* How much lead time will participants need? What's the best method for notifying them? What details do they need about the meeting?

- *Preparing materials, presentations, and activities.* What do you need to do to get ready for the meeting?

In the Appendixes you will find a Meeting Planning Worksheet you can use to answer all these questions. But first, let's examine each part of the planning process in more detail.

## IDENTIFY THE PURPOSE AND OBJECTIVE

In the example that began this chapter, Marla had only a vague idea of her reasons for calling the meeting of her staff and of what she wanted the meeting to accomplish. Unfortunately, people often call meetings with even less clarity about purpose and objectives than Marla's. A department chair might hold a weekly faculty meeting whether or not there is anything of substance to discuss, simply because there has always been a regular weekly meeting in that department. An administrative manager might call a meeting on the spur of the moment because he thinks it's a good idea for people to get together from time to time.

Such meetings are likely to leave people grumbling about being asked to take time out of their busy schedules to attend a meeting for no good reason. To ensure that your meeting will use everyone's time productively, clearly identify your reasons for calling the meeting and the objectives you expect the meeting to accomplish.

## Why Are You Calling This Meeting?

Sometimes people call meetings without stopping to consider whether they could achieve the same results with a memo, e-mail message, phone call, or brief meetings with individuals. As mentioned in Chapter One, if the purpose is primarily to convey information, a meeting is needed only when people are likely to have questions that can be answered most efficiently in a group or when you want their comments and suggestions. For example, changes in the agenda for a conference could be communicated via e-mail, while changes to admissions practices should probably be presented in a meeting.

Avoid calling meetings simply to "get people together." Although many people enjoy socializing with their colleagues, others dislike being asked to attend meetings that are not absolutely necessary. A social evening or weekend picnic, where attendance is voluntary, can be a better way to build community.

On the other hand, meetings are essential when a group needs to be involved in problem solving, strategic planning, or decision making. In fact, those activities are difficult or impossible to accomplish without a meeting.

## What Is the Meeting Intended to Accomplish?

After verifying that there are valid reasons for holding the meeting, clarify the objectives that you expect the meeting to achieve and formulate a statement that will communicate them clearly to participants. Be as specific as you can. Vague goals are likely to result in a vague meeting.

Here are some examples of meeting goals when there is one specific topic to be addressed:

- Discuss applicants for the new tenure track position and select three candidates to interview

- Learn about the changes that will be made to the library database next fall

- Decide how to allocate professional development funds for the upcoming semester

For meetings with multiple topics, there will be multiple goals. Here is the set of goals for one of the regular weekly faculty meetings for a university department:

- Bring everyone up to date on the status of current projects

- Identify issues that need to be addressed within the next month

- Remind everyone about upcoming deadlines for university-required reviews

- Hear a proposal from another department about a jointly taught course

# DRAW UP A PRELIMINARY LIST OF AGENDA ITEMS

Once you know the purpose and objectives of the meeting, you're ready to develop a preliminary list of agenda items. This is not the agenda itself—it's only a preliminary list. Later, you will refine that list to create the meeting agenda.

Begin by listing all the topics, issues, and activities that need to be included for the meeting to achieve its objectives. Note anything about an item that will be useful as you prepare the final agenda. For example, here is the preliminary list of agenda items for a meeting called to decide how to allocate professional development funds:

> Recap — amount of money available, criteria for allocating (Toni)
> Proposals — summaries only; send out ahead of time
> Discussion — keep to half an hour
> Decision — try for consensus
> Keep in mind — decide by 3/17 or risk losing funds

You might need to gather information from meeting participants and others before you can even begin to draw up the preliminary list of agenda items. For instance, you might send out an e-mail several days ahead of time to ask what items the participants want to include. If the meeting includes presenters from another area, you will need to find out what they plan to cover and how much time they will need.

When you create the preliminary list of agenda items, don't worry about the sequence or whether an item is really necessary or whether you will have time to cover everything. Just make a list of all the topics, issues, and activities that might be needed to achieve the meeting objectives. You will decide how much time you need for each item, add or eliminate items, and establish the order later.

There is, however, one thing to do with the list before moving on to the next step in the planning process: go through it once and mark any item that *must* be addressed in the meeting, such as a time-sensitive decision. Identifying essential items now will be helpful later if you find that you will not have time to cover everything and need to decide what to drop.

# DECIDE HOW LONG THE MEETING WILL BE

It seems reasonable that a meeting's length be determined by the time needed to cover all the agenda items. But in the real world, meeting length is usually limited by the participants' schedules and the availability of the meeting space. It's no use scheduling a half-day meeting if several key participants cannot be available for half a day or you can only have the room for two hours.

If there are predetermined limits on the meeting time, your planning task will be to determine how many of the preliminary agenda items can be covered during that time. If there are no predetermined limits, your task becomes figuring out how long the meeting should be by estimating how much time you will need to cover all the items.

## Estimate the Time Carefully

Successful meetings are those that allow enough time to cover all the agenda items without people feeling rushed. Here are two serious problems that can result when there is too much to cover in the time available:

- *Only the items at the beginning of the agenda are given sufficient attention.* Other items are rushed through or even dropped, leaving people who are primarily interested in those items wondering why they bothered to come.

- *The meeting goes overtime.* People expect meetings to end when they are scheduled to end. If they don't, participants with other commitments will get up and leave; those who stay are likely to have their attention on the clock, not on the business at hand.

## Estimate the Time Needed for Each Agenda Item

Whether or not you already know how long the meeting will be, begin this part of the planning process by estimating the time that will be needed to cover each item on your preliminary list. Be generous in your estimates—things usually take more time than you expect, not less.

Of course, it can be difficult to decide how long a given item is likely to take. Think about your experience with similar items, either as a meeting leader or as a participant. How long does it usually take to deliver this kind of information, make this kind of decision, or discuss this kind of issue?

Here are some factors to consider:

- *How complicated is the item?* How long is it likely to take to present all the information so people will understand it? Will people need to ask a lot of questions?

- *How difficult is the decision?* Will it require a lot of discussion? Is the group likely to have difficulty reaching consensus?

- *How important is the item?* Is it worth spending a lot of time making sure all the information gets across and people can ask all their questions? Will the decision have far-reaching effects?

## When Meeting Length Is Limited

How much you can cover might be limited by an already established meeting time, the amount of time participants can be available, the availability of the meeting space, and other

factors. If the committee you chair meets from 12:00 to 2:00 on the first and third Wednesdays of the month for a brown-bag lunch, you will have to determine whether you can realistically cover all the agenda items in that two-hour meeting—including the time you'll need to open and close the meeting. If the room is only available from 11:00 to 12:30, the agenda can include only what can be realistically covered in an hour and a half.

If everything on your preliminary list of agenda items fits neatly into the time you have available, you can breathe a sigh of relief and continue with the planning process. But if there is not enough time or it looks as if the time will be tight, revise the preliminary agenda before proceeding, because eliminating topics or activities impacts the rest of your planning. Dropping an informational item or the discussion of a report might mean that certain people will not have to attend. Leaving out a presentation might mean that you do not need to order audiovisual equipment and can use a different room setup.

To decide which agenda items to keep and which to drop, revisit the meeting objectives. Ask yourself, "What's really important for this meeting? What could we do in another meeting or in another way?" Instead of one meeting, you might have two, each with a different set of participants. You might send out a report and gather comments through an e-mail discussion instead of in a meeting.

## When Meeting Length Is Unlimited

It's a little easier to plan when there are no predetermined limits on the meeting time, because your estimate of how long it will take to cover all the items on the preliminary agenda determines the length of the meeting. If your calculations show that you'll need two hours, including opening and closing segments, then the meeting will be two hours long. If the total estimate shows that you need six hours, including the opening, the closing, and breaks, that's how long your meeting should be.

Be careful, however. Always consider how long you can realistically expect participants to spend at a meeting. You might be able to cover all your agenda items in a four-hour meeting, but people might find it difficult to concentrate toward the end of that time. Depending on the situation, two shorter meetings might be better.

## Taking Breaks

It's important to remember that people need breaks. Breaks not only let people stretch and go to the restroom, they offer an opportunity for everyone to think about or chat with one another about the issue under discussion and, perhaps, return with some fresh ideas.

Schedule a break after each ninety minutes to two hours of meeting time. After a break, allow five minutes of slack time in the schedule for people to get back into the room and settle down—in other words, leave fifteen minutes in the agenda for a ten-minute break.

For lunch meetings, people need ten minutes or so to get settled and begin eating. After lunch, it's a good idea to give people a break of at least fifteen or twenty minutes to freshen up, take a brisk walk, and so on.

# DECIDE WHOM TO INVITE

Here are the two questions to answer when drawing up the list of people to invite: Who *must* be there for the meeting to achieve its objectives? Who else should be invited and why? To answer these questions, take another look at your meeting objectives and the preliminary list of agenda items.

## Who Must Be at the Meeting?

Think about who needs to be present for the meeting to achieve its objectives. It's essential to include people who:

- Have key information to disseminate

- Need the opportunity to ask questions about or comment on information that will be disseminated

- Have the knowledge, expertise, or sense of ownership needed to resolve problems that will be discussed

- Must be involved in any decisions that are to be made

## Who Else Should Be Invited and Why?

There are a number of reasons for inviting people whose presence is not essential to the business at hand. Generally, you might want to invite people who:

- Have some interest in the topics or issues

- Might be able to make helpful contributions to the discussion

- Might have useful information or perspectives to provide

You might also invite certain people to foster a sense of community and certain others because the politics of the situation demand their inclusion. But take care when inviting nonessential participants. People who are not really involved in the business of the meeting can be distracting and disruptive. Also, make sure that people who are not key participants know that their presence is voluntary and have enough information about what the meeting will cover to decide whether they want to attend.

## How Large Should a Meeting Be?

Meetings can be any size, of course, but the types of everyday meetings we're focusing on in this book generally have from six to thirty participants. A meeting of fewer than six people is generally more impromptu

*The Jossey-Bass Academic Administrator's Guide to Meetings*

and requires less planning than a larger meeting, although planning never hurts. Meetings with more than thirty people usually require a little more planning as well as more careful facilitation. For example, question-and-answer sessions need to be managed more carefully in larger groups to make sure that they do not take up all your time; the discussion and decision-making process also needs to be more carefully structured, perhaps by breaking the group down into smaller discussion groups.

# CHOOSING THE TIME AND PLACE

It's not always easy to find a good time to hold a meeting in an academic setting because people's schedules vary so widely and many of them are too busy for meetings at certain times of the year. Also, many people are away from campus for weeks or months at a time.

Finding a meeting room that can be set up in the right way, is the right size, in the right location, and available at the right time can also be difficult. Even though campuses are filled with meeting places (classrooms), conference rooms are often at a premium.

But it's worth the effort to find the right time and the right place—the meeting time and the setting can have a significant impact on meeting success.

## Factors to Consider About Meeting Time

Have you ever announced a meeting only to find that key participants can't be available at that time? If so, then you know the frustration of having to reschedule and notify everyone of the new meeting time. That won't happen if you check with key participants to see when they are available before scheduling the meeting. For example:

- Call people or send out an e-mail saying that you are arranging a meeting of a certain length about a certain topic and suggest three possible meeting times

- Ask people to tell you when they are *not* available for a meeting during a certain week

- Ask members of your group to give you their preferred meeting times

It's important not to assume that key people will be there even if the group meets on a regular schedule. People take vacations. They travel on university business. They attend conferences. You won't be able to discuss the budget at your next staff meeting if the person who has been assembling the budget figures is on a sailboat in the Caribbean.

When scheduling meetings, also consider the many other events that may be taking place at the institution and in people's professional lives. Here are some guidelines:

- Avoid times of the year when people are especially busy, such as the first and last weeks of a term and finals week.

- In general, avoid Friday afternoons, the day before a holiday, nights, and weekends unless the group has indicated a willingness to meet at those times.

- On most campuses, avoid scheduling meetings that involve faculty during the summer and holiday periods, simply because people won't be around. On the other hand, summers and holidays are sometimes excellent times for administrative staff to meet because things are quieter.

## Factors to Consider About Meeting Place

Carefully consider the characteristics of the meeting room and the room's location. Is the room large enough? Light enough? Quiet enough? Convenient enough? Cramped quarters distract people by making them uncomfortable; noise from the other side of a room divider make it hard for people to hear presenters and one another; a location that forces too many people to travel too far might mean that people come late or leave early.

Here are some guidelines for choosing a meeting place:

- *The room should be large enough for the group.* Participants should be able to sit comfortably in a seating arrangement that allows them to see one another, the facilitator, and any presenters. If the room is very large and the group small, use only one end.

- *The space should be private.* One end of an office or an arrangement of chairs in a lounge might be okay for a brief, impromptu meeting on a subject that does not require privacy. But it is not satisfactory for most meetings. People are less willing to discuss issues freely when they think that other people might be listening, especially if the topics are confidential or sensitive.

- *The space should be free from distractions.* External or internal noise, interruptions, and even the ringing of an unanswered telephone can make it hard for people to concentrate.

- *The room should be yours for the duration of the meeting.* To avoid cutting a meeting short or scrambling to find another space at the last minute, double-check scheduling arrangements to be sure that another group is not planning to use the room until your meeting is over.

- *The location should be convenient.* If possible, bring the meeting to the people instead of bringing the people to the meeting. If people are coming from various locations, choose a room that is easily accessible for the majority of the participants. For example, if most of the participants work at a satellite campus, hold the meeting there instead of at the downtown center. If everyone works on the same campus but in different buildings, look for a centrally located room for the meeting.

- *The space should be neutral.* Holding a meeting in a place not perceived as belonging to the convener can help establish a sense of ownership of the issues among participants.

## Seating Arrangements

Set up the room in a way that encourages the open exchange of ideas. Avoid classroom-style seating, where people sit in rows facing the facilitator (it's not even the best arrangement for a class). Instead, arrange seat-

> ## THE CARE AND FEEDING OF MEETING PARTICIPANTS
>
> Eating and drinking can relax people and help them interact more readily. If possible, provide beverages such as coffee, tea, juice, and bottled water. For morning meetings, people appreciate a continental breakfast with fruit, bagels, or sweet rolls; in the afternoon, participants will opt for juice or soft drinks and snacks, such as pretzels or chips. For regular meetings, the responsibility for providing food might be rotated among participants.
>
> For meetings that include lunch or dinner, keep in mind that the food is not the purpose of the meeting, so it should be simple, easy to serve, and easy to eat.

ing so that people can easily see and hear one another, the facilitator, and any presenters, and so that each participant feels that he or she is an integral part of the group.

See the Appendixes for several suggested seating arrangements.

## PREPARING THE AGENDA AND NOTIFYING PARTICIPANTS

The agenda is the meeting's working plan. It specifies the time, place, and duration of the meeting; what items will be covered and in what order; who is making presentations or leading discussions; and what actions will be taken at the meeting. Be sure to send out the agenda far enough in advance so participants can prepare themselves for the meeting.

What should an agenda include? The way you set up an agenda is up to you. But most agendas include the following:

- Date of the meeting, including the day of week

- Time the meeting will begin and end

- Location, including a map if people are likely to be unfamiliar with the location

- Names of convener, facilitator (if different), and presenters (if any)

- Purpose and objectives of the meeting

- The order of agenda items and who will present or facilitate each item

- The start and end times for each item (especially important for outside presenters, who need to know when to arrive and how long they will have the floor)

- For each agenda item, whether the item is for information only, for discussion only, for discussion and a decision, and so on

- What people need to do to prepare for the meeting, such as read a report (when sending out the agenda, include any documents people need to read ahead of time, or tell them how to obtain the documents)

- What people need to bring to the meeting, such as notes, materials for distribution, ideas, their calendars, and so forth

- Whom to contact if people have questions or a time conflict

## A Task-Focused Agenda

To help people focus on what they will be doing at the meeting, state each agenda item as an objective or a task instead of a topic. For example, expand the topic of conference planning into a statement: "Develop a preliminary plan for the conference, including the theme, key topics, dates, and location. Set up a conference committee to handle detailed planning."

## Notifying Participants

If people already know about the meeting, you can use the agenda as the means of notification. If they do not already know, you might want to send out a preliminary memo with the date, time, place, and meeting objectives, and ask people to let you know right away if they have a scheduling conflict. Then send out the agenda at least two or three days before the meeting, earlier if people will need more time to prepare.

## Meeting Without a Prepared Agenda

Occasionally, a meeting has no prepared agenda, only a topic and an objective. An office manager might call an impromptu staff meeting to brainstorm suggestions for handling the work of a key staff member who unexpectedly resigned. A department chair might call a special meeting to discuss preliminary responses to a new program review requirement.

Without an agenda, however, a meeting can easily get off track, so the first thing the group needs to do is create one. The meeting leader or facilitator should clarify the meeting's objectives. Then the group can take a few minutes to list on a flip chart page the questions they need to answer, issues they need to address, and priorities they need to establish, and then decide how much time to allot to each item. For a sample Agenda Worksheet, see the Appendixes at the end of this book.

# CHOOSING A FACILITATOR AND RECORDER

At some point in the planning process, you need to decide whether you will facilitate the meeting yourself or ask someone else to facilitate. Also, you need to decide who will handle the recording responsibilities.

If you choose not to facilitate yourself, involve the facilitator in the planning process as early as possible, especially if the person comes from outside the group. The more information the facilitator has, the more able he or she will be to run a successful meeting. Be sure to provide background information about the group, including anything the facilitator needs to know about the group dynamics. If the group is about to tackle a sensitive, complex, or otherwise difficult issue, choose someone who has good facilitation skills and experience with similar groups.

As mentioned in Chapter Two, the recorder can be a member of the group or someone who is not directly involved in the business at hand. In either event, the recorder and facilitator need to work closely together to decide on the recording methods. The recorder needs a copy of the agenda and a list of participants.

## PREPARING FOR THE MEETING

The final step in the planning process is to identify what materials, presentations, and activities need to be prepared ahead of time. While many of these tasks can be handled by an administrative support person, it is important for you and the facilitator to oversee the process to ensure that everything gets done on time and correctly.

Depending on the meeting, you might need to prepare or arrange for all or some of the following:

- Sufficient copies of materials that will be handed out to meeting participants

- Flip chart pages, slides, or overhead transparencies with all or some of the following:

    Objectives
    Agenda
    Key points of information items
    Key points of proposals or problems
    Questions and issues that need to be addressed

- Presentations, including prepared flip chart pages, slides, or video

- Activities to help people develop solutions to problems or arrive at consensus decisions

- Equipment and supplies, such as computers, slide projectors, flip chart easels, and marking pens

- Refreshments

See the Appendixes for a Meeting Preparation Checklist.

# WHAT'S NEXT

In this chapter, you have examined the reasons for planning meetings and the steps needed to plan a successful meeting. In the next chapter, you will find guidelines for facilitating a meeting so that it stays on track and accomplishes its objectives.

# 4

# Facilitating a Meeting

**W**HAT HAPPENED TO THE TIME?"

This was the day the English department faculty had to decide how to use the funds that had been allocated next semester for travel and guest lecturers. But the meeting was halfway over, and they had discussed only three of the six proposals that had been submitted. Each time they began to talk about one of the proposals, someone would raise a side issue. For example, while they were discussing Sylvia's proposal to bring in several poets for a series of readings and workshops, Marlon wondered aloud "how in the world" one of the poets had been awarded a national prize, and the next fifteen minutes were spent critiquing the poet's work. Joellen, who was facilitating the meeting, looked at the clock in frustration. There was less than an hour left. If they didn't make the decision today, she'd have to call another meeting for later in the week—and then everyone would complain that they spent all their time in meetings.

## INTRODUCTION

Although Joellen is well aware that the meeting has gotten off track, she doesn't know what to do. And she's right—people will not be happy about being called to another meeting on the same topic. In fact, the people who are eagerly engaging in the discussion of side issues are the ones who will complain most loudly about having to spend time in another meeting.

Joellen needs to learn how to be a better meeting manager. Just as an instructor needs to manage a classroom so that the right amount of material is covered in a given time, a facilitator needs to manage the meeting so that the agenda items are covered adequately. For example, to keep this department meeting on track, Joellen needed to refocus people's attention on the discussion of the proposals every time someone brought up a side issue.

A good facilitator knows how to help a meeting run smoothly and achieve its objectives by making sure that it meets the criteria we have covered in earlier chapters:

- The meeting starts and ends on time
- People know why they are there and what they are trying to achieve
- The group stays focused on the agenda
- Ideas, concerns, and decisions are recorded accurately
- The time is used productively
- Things move along
- People know what is being said and decided
- People are clear about what happens next

In this chapter, we will look at actions and strategies that experienced facilitators have found help them run meetings that fulfill these criteria.

## HOW TO GET STARTED ON TIME

When the American Conservatory Theatre first came to San Francisco, they did something that was almost revolutionary at the time: they insisted on starting performances at the scheduled time. Latecomers were not seated until the intermission. It was not long before people got the idea.

It turned out that theatergoers had developed the habit of coming late because they knew from experience that performances usually started late. That's the same reason people develop the habit of coming late to meetings—when they do arrive on time, they have to sit around and wait for everyone to show up before the meeting finally begins.

To make sure that all the agenda items can be covered and out of respect for the participants, one of a facilitator's most important—and most frustrating—jobs is getting the meeting started at the scheduled time. Here are some ways to get that job done:

- *Do your advance planning and arrive early.* Make sure you have planned for everything you need—scheduled the room, ordered equipment, made copies of handouts, and so on. On the day of the meeting, arrive early enough to make sure that everything will be ready when participants arrive. Set up flip charts. Post wall charts. Rearrange the seating, if necessary. Test the equipment to make sure that it is functioning— meetings can be derailed by something as simple as a burned-out light bulb. By the time people come into the room, you should be all set up and ready to go.

- *Make sure everyone knows when the meeting is supposed to start.* People have a lot on their minds. Even though the agenda clearly states the start time for the meeting, it can be helpful to send out a reminder a day or two in advance. Include the meeting time, the purpose, the location, and anything participants need to bring, as shown in the example.

TO:     Film Department Faculty

RE:     Tomorrow's meeting

A reminder—we're meeting tomorrow (Thursday) at 4 p.m. in Room 603 to discuss how to allocate travel and guest lectureship funds. Bring your ideas and a snack to share. See you there.

- *If possible, make the room—and refreshments—available ten or fifteen minutes ahead of time.* For some people, socializing is an important part of a meeting. Try to make it possible for those people to get their socializing out of the way before the meeting begins. When you send out the agenda—and the reminders—make sure everyone knows what's socializing time and what's meeting time: "Come at 3:45 for coffee and snacks. The meeting begins promptly at 4 p.m."

- *Get started within a few minutes of the scheduled start time, even if everyone isn't there.* This strategy is difficult to carry out, especially the first few times you use it. In fact, you might have to begin two or three meetings with only a few of the participants present before people get the idea. But it is unfair to the people who make an effort to come on time to make them wait, and if you start late, you might run out of time before you've finished everything that needs to be done. It's worthwhile to establish the expectation that meetings will begin at the scheduled time.

If people are in the habit of coming late to meetings, try these strategies for changing their behavior:

- *Close the door.* It's easy to slip into a room with an open door. But a closed door needs to be opened, calling attention to the latecomer's entrance.

- *Set up the seating so that latecomers have to sit in a prominent place.* Vacant chairs at the back of the room make it easy for latecomers to slip in unnoticed. The discomfort of having to move into a conspicuous seat while the meeting is going on can motivate people to come earlier the next time.

- *Make sure the meeting time is as convenient as possible.* Do people need to run all the way across campus from a class to get to the meeting on time? Do they have to arrive on campus much earlier than usual? Find out as much as possible about people's schedules and plan meeting times accordingly.

- *Make sure people know why their presence is important.* People sometimes drift into meetings late because they don't think it's important for them to be there. The agenda should clearly show people will miss something important if they are not there when the meeting begins.

- *Turn the problem over to the group.* Meetings that continually start late affect everyone. So put the problem on the agenda for discussion, work together to find the underlying causes, and come up with mutually agreeable solutions.

# HOW TO OPEN THE MEETING

Most people come to meetings hard on the heels of another activity. When they enter the room, their attention may still be on that activity. They need to make a transition from the earlier part of their day to the meeting.

Experienced facilitators know that it is worth taking the time to open a meeting in a way that helps people make that transition, prepares them to focus on the business of the meeting, and establishes the meeting tone and expectations. In fact, what happens during the first few minutes can affect the success of the entire meeting.

Here are some ways for getting meetings started:

- *Facilitate introductions.* People are uncomfortable not knowing anything about the other people in the room. Unless people already know one another, ask the participants to introduce themselves, perhaps with a brief statement about why they are there. Even for regularly scheduled meetings, take a few minutes for introductions whenever there is anyone new in the room.

- *Review the purpose and objectives of the meeting.* Everyone should have the same understanding of why the meeting was called and what the meeting is intended to achieve. For some meetings, you might want to post the purpose and objectives on the wall.

- *Review the agenda, including the time allotted for each item.* Point out any changes that have been made since the agenda was distributed. If possible, post the agenda where it is easy to see and refer to during the meeting.

- *Describe the expected "products" of the meeting,* such as decisions, action items, or key points for a report. Knowing where they are going makes it easier for people to get there.

- *Establish ground rules.* Certain agreed-upon rules can help meetings run more smoothly. A ground rule might be that after someone speaks, that person must wait for at least one, and perhaps two, more people to speak before speaking again. Another might be that silence is not to be interpreted as agreement. Still another might be that what is said in the room stays in the room, unless everyone agrees that it can be revealed. What ground rules you need depend on the situation and the nature of the group; what's important is that the group itself come up with and agree on the ground rules.

**Examples of Ground Rules**

> Come on time—and come prepared
>
> What is said in this room stays in this room
>
> Decisions will be made by consensus unless group votes to exempt
>
> Anyone can call for a check-in at any time
>
> Focus on content, not personalities
>
> Respect other points of view, even if you disagree

## Opening Activities

For some meetings, an opening activity helps people feel comfortable and engages them in the business at hand. For example, you might want an opening activity when:

- People do not know one another

- People are likely to have strong feelings about the issues that are being addressed

- There are tensions in the group

- The primary purpose of the meeting is to generate ideas

Here are examples of opening activities:

- *"Tell me about yourself."* Give each person a minute or so to tell the group whatever she wants to divulge about herself: "I have been a professor of art history for sixteen years, I have three children, I go rock climbing on the weekends." In a large group, people can do this activity in pairs.

- *"What do you expect from today?"* Ask each person to state one expectation for the meeting: "I would like to know what everyone thinks are the primary objectives of the conference we're planning."

- *"What's one idea?"* Ask each person to come up with one idea—whether for solving a problem, updating a program, or improving a procedure or system.

- *"What is one concern you have about today?"* Ask each person to share one concern they have about the meeting that is about to begin: "I'm afraid that we won't be able to agree on how to . . ."

## How to Stick to the Agenda

In the story that begins this chapter, Joellen was unable to keep the group focused on the agenda, with the result that they did not have time for the most important agenda item—the decision about how to allocate the funds. Keeping the group from wandering away from the agenda and making sure that all the agenda items are covered are two of the facilitator's most difficult—and most essential—responsibilities.

Try the following methods for helping the group stick to the agenda:

- *Avoid packing an agenda with back-to-back items.* Leave some slack time for transitions between items. Also leave time for wrapping up discussions.

- *Keep presentations to a reasonable length.* Presenters should know that they must use their time to present what group members need to know, not every detail about the topic. Make sure all the presenters know how much time they have and that their presentations will be stopped when the time has run out. Include sufficient time on the agenda for questions or a discussion after each presentation.

- *At the beginning of the meeting, post the agenda—with the times allocated to each item—where participants can see it easily.* Draw participants' attention to the posted agenda as needed to help them focus on where they are in the meeting process.

- *Keep an eye on the time.* Prompt presenters as needed to ensure that they know their time is about to run out. Let participants know when a discussion is nearing the end of its allotted time or when they are nearing the end of the time allocated for making a decision.

- *Acknowledge new issues and concerns as they come up, record them on a flip chart page, and leave time at the end of the meeting to deal with them:*

"That's an important issue, Frank, but we had not planned to talk about it today. Let's write it down [with a nod to the recorder], and before we leave today we can decide when to address it."

- *If you think a discussion is getting off track, guide people back to the agenda:* "That's an interesting subject, Jamie, but right now we're talking about . . . "; "Flavio, I'm not sure how that point relates to [topic]"; [To the group] "We seem to be off target here. Let's take another look at what we're trying to do."

- *If the group seems to be finished with a topic, review the key points from the discussion, then ask, "Does anyone have anything to add?"* If a discussion seems to be covering the same ground, suggest that the group move on: "It seems to me that we've covered that issue, so unless someone has something new to add, let's go on to . . ."

- *If you are not finished with an agenda item but are running out of time, stop.* Summarize the key points of the discussion so far. Then ask the group whether they want to drop the item, drop another item to make time for expanding the discussion, or put the item on the agenda for the next meeting.

## When to Close a Discussion

Discussions need to be brought to a close when they are no longer serving the purpose of the meeting. Here are several indications that a discussion should be closed:

- People are starting to repeat points that have already been covered and no one has anything new to add

- Agreement has been reached or it is clear that agreement cannot be reached

- The group needs more information to be able to address a specific issue

- It becomes clear that people not present at the meeting need to be involved in the discussion

- People need more time to think about or research the issue

- People have become upset and need time to cool down

- It becomes clear that the issue concerns only a few people who need to discuss it outside of the meeting

- It becomes clear that changes in the situation either make the issue irrelevant or make it unproductive to discuss at the moment

## When to Discard the Agenda

Occasionally it becomes clear that the agenda is not serving the group's most immediate and important needs. When that seems to be happening, call for a pause in the proceedings to discuss the situation and decide what to do. The decision to drop agenda items or the agenda itself should be the entire group's, not the facilitator's alone.

Here are some of the situations in which you might need to discard the agenda:

- A very important agenda item that needs to be addressed immediately turns out to be much more complicated than it first appeared, requiring more of the group's time

- During a discussion, a new issue comes up that needs to be addressed immediately

- There has been a change in the situation or there is new information that affects all or some of the items on the agenda

- It becomes clear that the group is not functioning effectively and needs to focus on its own dynamics before it can get any useful work done

# CAPTURING ESSENTIAL INFORMATION

In a successful meeting, the recorder and the facilitator work closely together to make sure that essential information is captured. The nature of their relationship depends in part on whether the recorder takes notes quietly from within the group or stands in front of the room writing on a flip chart. But the goal is the same—to capture the following:

- The names of the people present at the meeting

- Key points from participants' discussions

- Important ideas, concerns, and issues that participants raise

- The decisions participants make and the way in which each decision was reached (vote, consensus, and so on)

- Action items, including timetables, and individuals responsible for
each item

- Issues and topics identified for the next meeting

## Recorder Seated Among the Group

A recorder seated among the group or off to the side is acting as a passive
note taker. It's important to check in with the person from time to time
to make sure that he captures important points: "Alan, did you get Suzie's
point about . . ." Although the recorder should know that he can ask
people to clarify or repeat something they said, it helps when you take a
moment to repeat or summarize key information.

Once in a while, you might ask the recorder to read his notes aloud.
This can be especially helpful before the group makes a decision. It can
also be helpful if there seems to be a misunderstanding about something.

It's important that the recorder understand that he is not responsible
for writing down everything that people say but for capturing the key
points. Otherwise, the person might be writing so fast that he is unable
to listen carefully enough to get the gist of a discussion or recognize when
something is not clear.

Notes taken in this way are usually distributed after the meeting in the
form of minutes.

## Recorder Standing in Front of the Group

As we mentioned in Chapter Two, there are several advantages to having
the recorder write on flip chart pages that everyone can see. People feel
assured that what they have said has been heard. They can quickly spot
and correct errors or omissions. The pages can be posted around the room

to help keep people focused on the topic. Flip chart pages are especially helpful during the decision-making process because they can be referred to again and again.

Standing in front of the group, however, can put the recorder in the position of competing with the facilitator for people's attention. The recorder should speak only to ask for clarification or a summary, leaving the focus on the facilitator as she guides the group through the agenda.

After the meeting, the recorder or the facilitator needs to collect the flip chart pages and type them up for distribution to participants and others who need to know what took place at the meeting.

# HOW TO FACILITATE A PRODUCTIVE DISCUSSION

As everyone who has ever attended a meeting knows, a discussion can be engaging, focused, and productive, or it can drag on and on, with nothing much being said. In some meetings, all the participants involve themselves in the discussions; in others, most people sit passively while only a few talk. Sometimes group members come up with creative solutions to disagreements and problems, and sometimes they leave the meeting feeling that nothing has been accomplished.

For a meeting to be successful, the facilitator must encourage active participation and keep the discussion focused on the topic. Here are some ways to achieve these goals:

• *Create an atmosphere where people feel comfortable speaking up.* People will only speak their minds when they feel confident that their ideas will be listened to respectfully and taken seriously. Acknowledge the ideas that come up—no matter how unworkable an idea might seem, the individual deserves respect for voicing it. Disagreement is fine, but do not allow anyone in the group to "shoot down" other people's ideas.

• *Ask open-ended questions.* As any experienced instructor knows, asking a question that can be answered with a yes or a no usually elicits a correspondingly brief reply:

*Question:* "Anne, do you think that we should host the conference next spring?"

*Response:* "Sure."

To elicit more information, ask the question in such a way that the respondent needs to provide more information:

*Question:* "Anne, what do you think would be the advantages of our hosting the conference next spring?"

*Response:* "For one thing, we wouldn't have to travel ourselves. And we'd get a lot of recognition. . . ."

• *Use brainstorming.* To encourage the group to come up with ideas, possible solutions to problems, and so on, use a brainstorming process in which generating ideas is separated from evaluating them. See Chapter Five for more on brainstorming.

---

## TIPS FOR RECORDING ON FLIP CHART PAGES

Here are some techniques for using flip chart pages effectively to record what takes place at a meeting:

• Avoid sentences—focus on key words and phrases.

• Summarize and abbreviate, but use the participants' own words.

• Ask people to repeat and clarify as needed.

• When there is a lot to write down—during a brainstorming session, for example—ask for a helper to write on a second flip chart.

• Print in clear, legible letters.

• Don't worry about spelling or punctuation.

• Number each sheet.

• Post pages when they are filled.

• Use symbols—arrows, circles, asterisks—to link points and show emphasis.

• Use different colors to highlight and separate points.

• Use bold colors—blue, green, black—with red and orange for emphasis, and avoid yellow, which cannot be seen clearly.

• Throw pens away when the ink runs low.

---

- *Recognize that people participate in different ways.* Some people demonstrate their involvement in the meeting by speaking up often, but others speak only when they feel they have something very important or relevant to say. If people are remaining silent, pay attention to their body language to see whether they are following the discussion.

- *Respect differences in communication styles.* Differences in personality and culture mean differences in the way people communicate. Many people were raised to consider it impolite to interrupt when others are speaking, put forward their own point of view, make direct eye contact with others when speaking, or speak forcefully. Those people will naturally speak less and less forcefully in meetings than people who feel perfectly comfortable jumping in and stating their own opinion.

- *Give everyone an opportunity to speak.* If one or two people tend to dominate the discussion, find ways to encourage others to speak. There are some suggestions below.

## How to Encourage Participation

If only a few people at your meetings do all the talking, try these strategies:

- *Establish a ground rule that encourages people to take turns:* once a person has spoken, she has to wait until one or two other people have spoken before speaking again.

- *Pose an open-ended question to the group*—"What's one concern you have about the new procedure?"—and ask each person to respond in no more than three sentences. Note: When asking people to respond one by one, always allow people the option of passing.

- *Be patient.* Not everyone has what they want to say on the tip of their tongue. If someone wants to speak but is having difficulty articulating what he wants to say, wait before jumping in and saying it for him. If he is really having trouble, a prompt might help: "Leo, are you concerned about how Meg's proposal fits into our long-term plans for . . . ?"

- *Recognize the value of silence.* Some people need a few moments to collect their thoughts after a question has been asked. Pose a question, then ask the group to pause for five to ten seconds before responding. Or ask the group to wait for five to ten seconds before responding to something someone else has said.

• *Before beginning a discussion, ask people to write down their initial comments.* For example: "You've all read the task force report. Before we discuss it, let's take two minutes to write down one to three points you would like to make about it." Then go around the room and ask everyone to share one point from their list.

• *For a larger group, ask people to discuss an issue in small groups of three to five people.* Then ask each group to report the key points from their discussion to the larger group.

## How to Ensure That Participants Understand Announcements and Decisions

The fly on the wall at a typical meeting might notice that at some points, people turn to their neighbors with quizzical expressions and ask, "What did he say?" or "So did we decide to . . . ?" That confusion happens not because people aren't paying attention but because things are moving too quickly and the facilitator is not doing enough to summarize and clarify what's being said.

When people read a book, a journal article, or a report, they can turn back and reread something that is not clear. Most chapters or sections begin with an overview that lets readers know what to expect and end with a summary that reminds them of the key points that were covered. At a meeting, participants depend on the facilitator to provide the overview, the summary, and any reviewing or clarification that might be needed.

Here are some ways to help participants follow what is being said and decided:

• *At the beginning of a discussion, summarize and clarify the question or issue and give people a chance to ask questions before launching into the discussion:* "The university is planning to allocate $5,000 next semester to each of ten departments that come up with the best proposals for using the funds. You've all read the guidelines. What we need to do today is come up with ideas so that Lorraine and Brad can draft a proposal. But first, does anyone have questions about the guidelines or what we're trying to do?"

- *During a discussion, summarize and clarify what people say as needed:* "If I've got it right, Parker is concerned that high-profile projects will take precedence over projects with more long-term value to the department."

- *When the discussion is finished, summarize key points and decisions before moving on:* "Let's review the ideas we've come up with and see whether anyone has anything to add."

## Common Facilitation Problems

We all know these people: they start side conversations, dominate the discussions, keep shifting off the topic, turn discussions into arguments, behave in negative or hostile ways, or make disparaging remarks when other people are talking. These "disrupters" can quickly ruin a good meeting—but what can you do about them?

The steps you take when someone's behavior becomes a problem depend on the nature of the behavior, how much of an effect it is having on the meeting, and other factors. For example, you might not jump in immediately if someone gives one overly long explanation or starts one side conversation. But you do need to step in right away if a group member continues to dominate the discussions, becomes openly hostile, insults someone else, or engages in other unacceptable behavior.

Here are some steps you can take to avoid behavioral problems or to reduce their effects when they do occur:

- *Help the group establish ground rules regarding behavior in the meeting.* One ground rule might state that people will not engage in side conversations. Another might limit comments to three minutes. Still another could say that group members agree to respect the validity of other people's perspectives, even if they do not agree. You can then invoke those rules as needed during the meeting: "Susan and Adam, could you remember our rule about side conversations?" "Filippo, could you wrap up your comments? You're just about at the three-minute limit." "Maritza, we agreed not to shoot down other people's ideas."

• *When disruptive behavior continues or becomes serious, take action promptly.* As mentioned above, you might ignore a negative remark or two, or a few interruptions. But if someone persists in behaving in a distracting or disruptive manner, it's important to take action. The longer the behavior continues, the more uncomfortable the group will be and the more difficult it will be to keep the meeting going smoothly.

• *Focus on the behavior, not the person.* Instead of saying, "Francine, do you have to be so rude?" try, "Francine, could you please save your comments until Harlan is finished explaining his proposal?"

• *Try to discover the reason for the distracting or disruptive behavior.* People might not realize that their behavior is causing a problem. Perhaps they resent being asked to attend the meeting in the first place. Maybe they feel as if their concerns are not being heard. Sometimes you can get to the root of the problem by saying something like, "Melanie, I notice that you made several comments to Julie while Robin was speaking. Did you have something you wanted to say to the group?"

• *If someone's behavior is causing a serious problem and you have already asked the person to stop, call a break.* Take the person aside and say something like, "Dominic, I know you have a lot to say about the issues we're discussing. But you are not leaving time for anyone else to speak. I have to ask you to hold your comments for a while and give other people a chance."

## CLOSING THE MEETING

Few meetings are finished the moment people walk out the door. At the least, people leave with things to think about. Most of the time they also leave with things to do. It's essential that everyone leave with a good understanding of what has taken place and what happens next.

## TIPS FOR TELECONFERENCING

In today's busy world, people sometimes attend meetings by phone. Here are some things to keep in mind if one or more of your meeting participants is on the phone:

- Make sure the connection is clear and the volume is loud enough for people in the room to hear the phone participants.
- Make sure all the group members have introduced themselves to the people on the phone.
- When someone speaks, ask the person to begin with his or her name: "This is Jamie. I'd like to suggest that . . ."
- Make sure that everyone speaks slowly and distinctly. Ask the phone participants to let you know if they need something repeated.
- Before the meeting, provide the phone participants with anything you plan to hand out to the group in the meeting room.
- Describe visuals for the people on the phone.
- Take extra care to summarize key points from a discussion before moving on— remember that the phone participants can't see the flip charts.
- If you haven't heard from the people on the phone for a while, check to see that they are still there and give them an opportunity to speak.
- Before closing a discussion, make sure that the phone participants have had an opportunity to share their thoughts.

Here is what needs to be done to close a typical meeting:

- Summarize what has taken place. Quickly review the key points from the discussions and the decisions that the group made. Ask people to let you—and the recorder—know if you have left anything important out.

- Go over action items. On a flip chart page, list everything that needs to be done and make sure that someone has taken responsibility for handling each item. Include a timetable. See Chapter Five for more about action items.

- Review the list, if any, of side issues and concerns that came up during the meeting and decide what to do about them.

- If there is going to be another meeting, schedule it and identify items that need to be on the agenda.

- If appropriate, conduct a brief closing exercise: go around the room and ask each person to say in one or two sentences how they thought the meeting went and what might be done to improve future meetings. Note: allow people the option of passing.

- If appropriate, ask participants to complete a meeting evaluation form to evaluate the meeting more extensively. There is a sample evaluation form in the Appendixes that you can adapt for your own situation.

## WHAT'S NEXT

This chapter provided a look at ways to facilitate a meeting so that it runs smoothly and achieves its objectives. The final chapter focuses on ways to help a group carry out one of the most important functions of a meeting: making decisions.

# 5

# Decision Making and Action Planning

S O *WHAT* DID WE DECIDE?"

"How did the meeting go yesterday?" Carlos asked Ted as they were waiting for their turn at the copy machine. Ted threw him a quizzical look. "You know," Carlos said, "the task force for the interdepartmental conference?"

"Oh, that meeting," Ted said. He shrugged. "You know meetings."

"So you got everything ironed out, the theme, the speakers, who's doing what?"

"Are you kidding?" Ted said. "We talked a lot. Threw out lots of ideas. But I've got to admit, I'm still not sure what we decided to do, or who's supposed to do what to make the whole thing happen. Maybe someone else knows."

## INTRODUCTION

The goal of the task force meeting was to make decisions about the conference and develop an action plan for carrying out those decisions. But if Ted left without a clear understanding of what decisions were made and who would do what to implement them, chances are that nothing much will get done. In fact, it's likely that another meeting will have to be held to figure out why nothing is happening.

Making decisions and coming up with action plans for implementing them is one of the key reasons for holding meetings. For such meetings to be successful, it is essential that the facilitator understand the different ways in which decisions are made, methods for helping a group make decisions, and the importance of developing a workable action plan. These are the topics that will be covered in this chapter.

# WAYS OF MAKING DECISIONS

Misunderstandings or lack of clarity about how decisions are made can result in muddled decisions that are difficult or impossible to implement. It's important to understand the different ways in which decisions are made so that you can choose the most effective decision-making method for your situation.

Here are ways in which a decision might be made:

• *A leader makes the decision and announces it to the group (autocracy).* Examples of decisions that the leader might make without consulting the group include:

A decision that needs to be made immediately to deal with a crisis

Administrative decisions, such as whether to submit a budget request for a new photocopier

Staff decisions, such as whether to recommend a secretary for promotion

This decision-making method can save everyone a lot of time when it is used appropriately. But it's important to distinguish between decisions that the leader can (and should) make herself and decisions that should be brought to the group. It's even more important not to confuse a decision that has already been made with one that is open for discussion. In fact, the only reason to announce such decisions in a meeting instead of a memo is to give the leader an opportunity to explain the reasons for the decision and let the group ask questions. Simply announcing a decision is not a good enough reason for holding a meeting.

• *A leader gathers input from the group, then decides (modified autocracy).* With this method, the leader makes the decision, but only after soliciting input from the group or from group members individually. Examples include:

> Collecting editing suggestions for a report the leader is submitting to Administration

> Planning a reception for newly admitted graduate students

Some decisions that are most appropriately made by the leader benefit from this decision-making method in two primary ways: the leader gets valuable ideas and information that help him make a better decision, and the group is more likely to support the decision, knowing that their points of view have been heard.

It's not always necessary—or desirable—to hold a meeting for the sole purpose of gathering input. The leader can speak to people individually, or solicit input via e-mail. Meetings for gathering input are useful mostly when everyone needs to be on the same page about the issue and when the leader thinks that discussing the issue in a group will result in better ideas. No matter how the input is gathered, however, it is still important not to confuse this kind of decision with one that the group itself makes.

• *The decision is made by default (nonworking democracy).* Too often, decisions are assumed to have been made by the group when what has really taken place is a kind of nonparticipation. Someone says, "Let's do it this way." The facilitator says, "Sounds okay to me" and looks around the room. People shrug or nod. Assuming that everyone is in agreement, the facilitator says, "Right. Let's move on."

Decisions that are made by default tend to be unclear and difficult to implement. People who do not agree with the decision are likely to resist or even sabotage it, even though they failed to speak up. Even people who do not disagree but who felt no sense of participation in the process are unlikely to give the decision much support.

To avoid default decisions, never assume that a decision has been made until the participants have confirmed that they understand it and are willing to abide by it. At the very least, say something like, "It seems that we have decided to accept Rosalie's proposal for . . . Is there anyone who disagrees? Anyone who would like further discussion?" If no one raises an objection but you get a sense that people are not fully comfortable with the decision, you might want to ask for an expression of agreement—you could call for a vote, or go around the room and ask everyone to say whether they agree.

• *The group makes the decision by voting (democracy).* Voting is probably the most common way of making decisions in groups. It is efficient, and when used properly, it involves everyone in the process.

The group itself can determine the specifics: how many people must be present (a quorum) for a vote to be valid; whether a simple majority, a two-thirds majority, or some other percentage of yea votes determines whether a proposal is accepted; the criteria by which a vote can be appealed or challenged.

When decisions are made by voting, it's important that enough time be given to the prevote discussion so that dissenters feel that their positions have been heard, understood, and taken seriously. That way, they are more likely to support the decision, even if they do not fully agree with it.

• *The group decides by consensus (community).* A primary reason for making decisions in meetings is to involve everyone in the decision-making process and gain everyone's commitment to the decision. The idea behind consensus decision making is that once the decision is made, all the group members agree willingly to support it—or at least, not to stand in the way of implementation—even those who do not agree with it completely.

The process of achieving consensus, however, can be time-consuming, and it requires a great deal of attention. For decisions that do not significantly impact everyone or have long-term effects, a group might prefer to make decisions by voting. But where it can be used, the consensus process generally results in decisions that are more likely to be implemented.

Because consensus requires that every member of the group agree to support or abide by the decision, consensus cannot always be achieved. Thus, the group needs a backup plan that specifies how a decision will be made if they are unable to reach consensus on a specific issue within a given amount of time.

You will learn more about how to use the consensus process later in this chapter.

# DECIDING WHICH DECISION-MAKING METHOD TO USE

Using the right decision-making process for the situation can have a significant effect on the successful functioning of a group. For example, a group that spends too much time trying to reach consensus on unimportant issues can easily become discouraged. On the other hand, a leader who makes all or most of the decisions and then tries to get the group to agree will find that people soon develop a "why bother?" attitude.

Here are some of the factors to consider when determining which decision-making method to use:

• *How much time do you have?* As mentioned above, consensus decisions take time. So, in fact, do any decisions that the group makes itself. Sometimes it is more efficient for the leader to make the decision, perhaps after soliciting input from individuals, and announce it.

• *How important is the decision, and how many people does it affect?* To respect the value of people's time, consider the importance of the decision that needs to be made. How significant and far-reaching is its effect likely to be? Minor decisions that affect few people for relatively short amounts of time are often best made by a leader or a small group, leaving meeting time for more important issues.

• *How much information and expertise do group members have?* It is neither fair nor practical to ask people to make a decision when they do not have enough information or the right background to have a good understanding of the issue. For example, few lay people have enough technical knowledge to be able to select the right computer program for a specific function. The members of the group might specify what they need the program to do and leave the decision about what program to purchase up to a technical expert.

• *How important is it that people support and abide by the decision?* Making a decision is one thing; carrying it out is another. Consider how much commitment (buy-in) is needed from group members. Think about what might happen if a disgruntled member decides to sabotage the decision. If full support and participation is needed, it is usually worth taking the time to use the consensus process.

## MAKING CONSENSUS DECISIONS

Almost everyone understands the voting process: someone poses the issue, the group discusses it, and then someone calls for a vote. If a predetermined number of the group members, such as a majority or two-thirds, votes yea, the decision is made. The people who voted no usually have no choice but to accept it, even if they disagree strongly.

Consensus is different, and it is often not clearly understood. Essentially, consensus on an issue has been achieved when all group members feel they have been heard, have reviewed their positions in light of the facts and other members' points of view, and are willing to support and/or abide by the decision even if they do not fully agree.

Here are some key characteristics of a consensus decision:

- The objective is to make a decision that best serves the group and that every member, even those who do not fully agree, is willing to accept.

- The consensus process takes place in an atmosphere that encourages free and open discussion, active listening, and respect for other people's points of view, no matter how divergent those views might appear to be.

- Recognizing that achieving consensus is not always possible, the group decides ahead of time what to do if consensus cannot be reached in a specific situation.

## Reasons for Consensus in an Academic Setting

The consensus decision-making process is useful in nearly every organization, from corporate boardrooms to community groups. It is particularly useful in academic settings because it builds a sense of teamwork and community among people who often do much of their work independently and whose needs and perspectives often differ significantly.

The consensus process:

- Encourages trust, tolerance, and understanding among members of the group

- Increases participation

- Helps the group reach better decisions by bringing in greater amounts of information, more ideas, and a diversity of perspectives

- Seeks opportunities to combine ideas

- Creates stronger support for decisions because everyone feels that their points of view have been heard and considered

## A Consensus Process

As with any group decision-making process, the group must first have a clear understanding of the issue and the desired outcome. They need enough information about the situation. Then they need to generate and discuss ideas until the best decision emerges.

Here are the steps:

1. *Clarify the issue.* To begin the process, the facilitator or the group member who is seeking the decision needs to make sure that everyone clearly understands the issue, the desired outcome, and why the issue is important. It is helpful to post the desired outcome—the objective—on a flip chart page where everyone can see it.

2. *Provide information.* Before coming up with ideas and discussing

them, people need to know about any limitations there might be on the outcome, what the stakes are, and anything else that might affect the kind of decision they ultimately make. For example, if the objective is to decide how to use funds from a grant, the group needs to know if there are any guidelines specifying how those funds can be used, deadlines for using funds, and what happens if the funds are not used by the deadline. Post the limitations where people can see them throughout the process.

3. *Generate ideas.* Using a brainstorming process (see p. 68), take whatever time is needed to generate ideas. At this point, ideas should simply be put forth and recorded, not discussed, not evaluated. Record the ideas on flip chart pages and post the pages as they are filled.

4. *Review the list of ideas.* Number the list of ideas and quickly review them. Eliminate those that everyone agrees are obviously unworkable: "The grant guidelines won't let us use numbers 7 and 12." Combine those that are obviously redundant: "Numbers 3, 6, and 15 all say . . ." If anyone comes up with a new idea during this step, add it to the list.

5. *Discuss alternatives.* During the discussion, encourage people to participate fully by evaluating each idea in terms of its ability to resolve the issue and achieve the desired outcome. Summarize and clarify as needed to make sure that each person's point of view is heard and understood. Add to the list any new ideas that come up.

It's important to be aware that as people discuss the issue, the statement of the issue itself might change. For example, during a discussion of how to use the funds from a grant, the group might redefine the issue as whether grant funds should be used for department-wide activities or individual research activities.

If the issue seems to be changing, and the change appears substantial, go back to Step 1 and begin the process again by restating the issue. In these situations, you might find that you have more than one decision to make.

6. *Eliminate and combine alternatives.* As the discussion proceeds, look for opportunities to narrow the list by eliminating alternatives that the group does not support and by combining other ideas to create new alternatives. As long as everyone remains focused on the objective—coming up with the best decision possible in the given circumstances—instead of holding fast to their own positions, it usually becomes clear what will work

and what won't. And people's concerns can often be satisfied if at least part of a rejected idea is incorporated into another alternative.

If the group seems to be stuck, try to find out why. For example, go around the room and give each person a few minutes to summarize his position and concerns, and explain his reasoning.

7. *Call for a consensus vote.* When the group seems to have reached an agreement, the facilitator or one of the group members can call for a consensus vote. Before the vote, clarify the decision the group is about to make and write it on a flip chart page.

When you call for the consensus vote, participants can do one of the following:

- State their agreement with the decision

- State that they accept and support the decision even if they do not fully agree

- State that even though they do not agree, they can accept the decision and will not stand in the way of its implementation

- State that they do not agree and cannot accept the decision

*Note:* It can be helpful to post this list so participants can see it when they decide how to respond to the call for a consensus vote.

As stated earlier in this chapter, consensus has been achieved when all of the participants are able to accept the decision, whether or not they fully agree with it. If *any* participant remains opposed, discussion continues until consensus is achieved or it becomes clear that the group cannot achieve consensus within the available time.

## Consensus Process Tips

- Begin the process with a proposal: "I propose that we hold a three-day off-campus faculty retreat next spring"; "The task force recommends that we establish a tutoring center to be staffed with volunteer graduate students."

- Make sure that everyone has a good understanding of any constraints there might be on the decision they reach: "We can't spend more than $5,000"; "The dean has to approve our decision before we can implement it."

- To combine alternatives, use language such as: "Sachiko's idea for a four-color brochure is a good one, but it would send us over budget. What if we . . ."

- Remember that *compromise* is not a dirty word. In fact, compromising can be an excellent way of coming up with a decision that serves everyone's needs to the extent possible in the situation: "Lars, what if we run the first part of the program the way you suggest but follow Marilyn's suggestions for the second—could you live with that?"

- Make sure that the consensus you achieve is a real consensus, not a situation where people agree to go along with a decision because they are unwilling to voice dissenting opinions. False consensus means that some people are likely to resist or even sabotage the decision. Make sure everyone has an adequate opportunity to be heard and that their concerns are taken seriously. If they then accept the decision, it should be because they understand that the decision is in the best interests of the group, not because they were coerced into agreeing in order to keep everybody happy.

## Brainstorming Guidelines

Brainstorming is a process that takes advantage of group dynamics to stimulate more ideas than one or two people might come up with on their own. After the topic or question has been clearly defined, people share their ideas freely. Each idea is written down, without comment or discussion. The ideas are not discussed until all the ideas are in.

Here are some ways to make the best use of the brainstorming process:

- Allow enough time after clarifying the issue or question to get people's ideas flowing. For example, after posing the question, give participants two to three minutes to write down every idea that comes to mind.

- Begin the process by going around the room and asking each person to contribute one idea (giving people the option of passing if they wish). Then let people call out ideas as they come. If the ideas come too fast and furiously, repeat them as needed for the recorder.

- Make sure that the recorder—and possibly a helper—writes down *every* idea, even if it's been said before. It's best to write the ideas on flip chart pages that can be posted when they are filled so everyone can see them and refer to them later.

- Allow absolutely no discussion, comments, or evaluation during the brainstorming process. The recorder or facilitator can ask a participant to repeat what he or she said, but that's it. If people begin to comment, say something like, "Alex, please hold your comment—we're just generating ideas right now. We'll evaluate them later."

- When the flow of ideas slows down, read the list aloud to the group to see whether new points or ideas come to people's minds.

- Help everyone participate. As the flow of ideas slows down, call on people who have not been contributing: "Marlene, do you have anything to add?"

- If participants come up with only a few ideas, stop the process and discuss the reasons. Perhaps the question or issue is not yet clear. Perhaps people are uncomfortable for some reason. Or perhaps the short list they generated is sufficient.

- If the brainstorming process is new to the group, try a warmup exercise. For example, generate ideas for a department party.

## If the Group Cannot Reach Consensus

The first step for handling situations when consensus cannot be reached takes place *before* the consensus process begins. The ground rules that govern the decision-making process for any group that intends to use consensus to make decisions should include a backup plan that specifies how decisions will be made when consensus cannot be reached. For example, the group might agree that a three-fourths vote of members present can exempt a decision from the consensus process and that exempted decisions will be decided by a majority or a two-thirds majority of the participants.

When it becomes clear that the group cannot achieve consensus on an issue because one or more participants cannot accept the decision, stop the process. Once the discussion is no longer productive, it's time to do something else. For example:

- Go back to the beginning. Examine the original proposal to see whether it might be modified to accommodate the dissenters' needs and concerns. Sometimes the removal or addition of a single element is enough.

- Ask the dissenter(s) to research the situation and come up with new alternatives for the group to consider at the next meeting. The group must then take those alternatives seriously and consider them with open minds.

- Agree to exempt the decision from the consensus process.

## ACTION PLANNING: MAKING SURE YOUR DECISIONS ARE CARRIED OUT

In the scenario that began this chapter, Ted described a meeting that ended without a clear action plan. Chances are, nothing significant will result from that meeting, and the next time the task force meets, they will have moved no closer to their goal of setting up the conference.

In Chapter Four, we mentioned that one of the things to do when closing a meeting is to go over your action items. Many of those action items will be the result of decisions the group makes during the meeting. Once a decision about *what* to do has been made, it is essential to figure out *how* that decision will be implemented. To make sure that those decisions are carried out, your agenda needs to include time for action planning at the end of each decision item and/or at the end of the meeting. Everyone should leave the meeting with a clear understanding of who will do what and by when, to carry out the decisions that were made.

For example:

- A decision to revisit a topic at the next meeting means that at least one person needs to take responsibility for bringing in new information.

- A decision to use grant money to develop a Web site means that someone needs to do the preliminary work needed to develop and bring Web site designs back to the group for discussion.

- A decision to offer a position to one of three applicants means that someone needs to contact all the applicants and prepare a hiring letter for the successful candidate.

The action plan should specify what will be done, what the results will look like, who will do what, and the date by which the action will be carried out. It should be realistic and workable—otherwise, it probably will not be carried out.

Developing an action plan includes determining what needs to be done, who will do it, and when the work will be completed. It helps to follow a systematic process, such as the one shown below. A summary of this process can be posted so the group can see it while they work.

1. *List all the tasks that need to be done to carry out the decision.* If your group has decided to develop a Web site, your list might include identifying the content to include, finding a Web designer, and working with the designer to develop preliminary designs.

2. *For each task, decide what the results will look like*—such as a content outline for the Web site, an experienced designer who will work within your budget and timeframe, and three preliminary designs by the next meeting.

3. *For each task, decide who will do what.* Make sure that people understand what responsibilities they are taking on and that they make a commitment to carrying them out. For example, one person might volunteer to handle the Web site project, or the group might decide to appoint a task force of three to four people to work on the project together.

4. *Work out a realistic deadline.* Make sure that the work can be done within your time frame, considering the responsible parties' other commitments and the availability of resources. It would probably be unreasonable, for instance, to expect the people working on the Web design project to find a designer and come up with preliminary designs by the next weekly meeting.

5. *Decide who will provide support as people carry out their responsibilities.* The people carrying out the tasks might need help obtaining resources or they might need advice if they run into problems. One person, who could be the group's leader or another member, needs to take on the responsibility for making sure that the people carrying out the tasks have what they need.

6. *Decide who will follow up.* The follow-up person might be the recorder (who keeps the list of who has agreed to do what), the group leader, the facilitator, or a member of the group. But one person who is not involved in the task itself needs to be responsible for following up each action item.

7. *Decide how the results will be communicated to the group.* For example, the preliminary Web site designs might be e-mailed to group members, who would then return them to the responsible parties with comments or be ready to discuss them in a scheduled meeting.

# CONCLUSION

This book began with a description of a weekly faculty meeting that participants considered a waste of their time. Suppose that the group's leader read this book and used the information to improve the department's meetings. If so, Jennifer and Tyrone's next conversation might be quite different.

"WHAT A GREAT MEETING!" On their way to the parking lot after their department's most recent meeting, Jennifer and Tyrone are astounded at how much the group accomplished. They discussed three proposals for new courses, selected a site for their annual retreat, set up a plan for meeting key university deadlines, and brainstormed ideas for solving an ongoing problem with the use of the faculty lounge. "I wouldn't have believed it if I hadn't been there," Tyrone said. "I'm glad I forced myself to come."

"Me, too. Strange—the meeting went so quickly, and there didn't seem to be a wasted moment. And Phil and Arlene didn't get into a single argument. That's my idea of how a meeting should be run. I didn't even have a moment to read the student papers I brought along!"

"I'd still prefer not to go to so many meetings," Tyrone added. "But at least I feel better about going if they're all as productive as this one."

As we said at the beginning, meetings provide an array of opportunities to pass along information, generate ideas, and help people work together to achieve shared objectives. Now it's up to you to use what you've learned in this book to make sure that your own meetings are productive enough to leave participants feeling that each meeting is worth their time.

# APPENDIXES

Meeting Planning Worksheet

Sample Seating Arrangements

Agenda Worksheet

Meeting Preparation Checklist

Sample Meeting Evaluation

# Meeting Planning Worksheet

Primary Purpose of Meeting: _____

_____

Primary Objective(s) of Meeting:

_____     _____

_____     _____

_____     _____

Issues and Topics to Include on Agenda:

_____     _____

_____     _____

_____     _____

_____     _____

Meeting Length: _____

Key Participants:

_____     _____

_____     _____

_____     _____

## Meeting Planning Worksheet, Page 2

Others to Invite:

_____          _____

_____          _____

_____          _____

Day and Time: _____

Location: _____

Facilitator(s): _____

Recorder(s): _____

What People Need to Receive and Do Before the Meeting:

_____          _____

_____          _____

_____          _____

What I Need to Do to Prepare for the Meeting:

_____

_____

_____

_____

# Sample Seating Arrangements

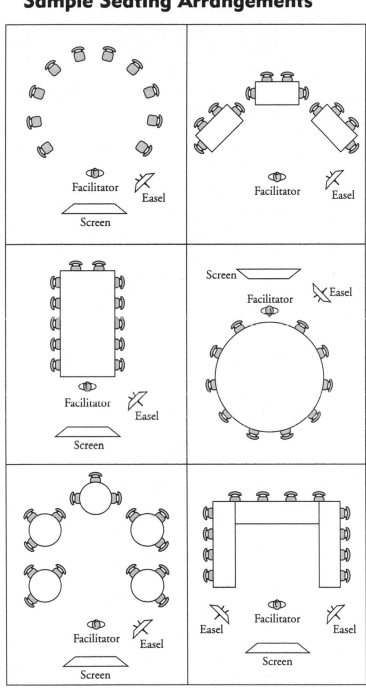

# Meeting Preparation Checklist

To prepare for a meeting, make sure that you, the facilitator, and/ or the administrative support person have considered or done the following:

☐ Notified participants

☐ Sent out the agenda and anything that participants need to read before the meeting far enough in advance for them to come prepared

☐ Confirmed with presenters that they will be there, be prepared, and know how much time they have

☐ Double-checked the room schedule and setup

☐ Double-checked arrangements for equipment such as overhead projectors or computers and arranged for technical support, if needed

☐ Arranged for a recorder and made sure that the recorder knows what's expected

☐ Made sufficient copies of anything the participants will receive during the meeting

☐ Arranged for paper and pens, refreshments, materials for activities, and so on

☐ Thought about how to open and close the meeting

☐ Prepared flip chart pages—showing the agenda, meeting objectives, and so forth—that need to be posted before people come into the room

☐ Thought about the best way to approach each agenda item. Do any items need special attention? A special introduction? Should the discussion begin in small groups? Is it likely to be difficult to reach consensus on an issue?

☐ Thought about how to handle potentially troublesome situations. Does one participant in this group tend to dominate the discussions? Is there someone who speaks up only when he has negative comments? Is there an issue that is likely to elicit strong emotions?

# Sample Meeting Evaluation

Meeting date: _____ Facilitator: _____

Circle the number that indicates the degree to which you agree with each statement. Write any comments you have on the lines provided for each statement. Write "N/A" next to any statement that does not apply to this meeting.

1. There was sufficient notice for this meeting.
   Disagree    1        2        3        4        5        Agree

Comments: _____

_____

2. The objectives for this meeting were clear.
   Disagree    1        2        3        4        5        Agree

Comments: _____

_____

3. The meeting achieved its objectives.
   Disagree    1        2        3        4        5        Agree

Comments: _____

_____

4. This meeting was a good use of my time.
   Disagree    1        2        3        4        5        Agree

Comments: _____

_____

5. The participants came prepared for the meeting.
   Disagree    1        2        3        4        5        Agree

Comments: _____

_____

6. The presenters were prepared.
   Disagree    1        2        3        4        5        Agree

Comments: _____

_____

7. The presentations were useful and relevant.
    Disagree    1       2       3       4       5       Agree

Comments: _____

_____

8. All the agenda items seemed important and relevant for the group.
    Disagree    1       2       3       4       5       Agree

Comments: _____

_____

9. The time was used efficiently.
    Disagree    1       2       3       4       5       Agree

Comments: _____

_____

10. The meeting stuck to the agenda.
    Disagree    1       2       3       4       5       Agree

Comments: _____

_____

11. The meeting started and ended on time.
    Disagree    1       2       3       4       5       Agree

Comments: _____

_____

12. The discussions were productive and focused on the topic at hand.
    Disagree    1       2       3       4       5       Agree

Comments: _____

_____

13. Everyone was given sufficient opportunities to participate in the discussions.
    Disagree    1       2       3       4       5       Agree

Comments: _____

_____

14. The room was comfortable and free from distractions.
     Disagree     1        2        3        4        5        Agree

Comments: _____

_____

15. The results of discussions were summarized and clarified before moving on to the next topic.
     Disagree     1        2        3        4        5        Agree

Comments: _____

_____

16. No single individual or group dominated the discussions.
     Disagree     1        2        3        4        5        Agree

Comments: _____

_____

17. People listened to one another.
     Disagree     1        2        3        4        5        Agree

Comments: _____

_____

18. People respected each other's viewpoints, even when they disagreed.
     Disagree     1        2        3        4        5        Agree

Comments: _____

_____

19. The decision-making process(es) we used was/were appropriate for the type(s) of decision(s) we made.

     Disagree     1        2        3        4        5        Agree

Comments: _____

_____

20. We left the meeting with clear action plans for what happens next, including who will do what to implement any decisions we made.

     Disagree     1        2        3        4        5        Agree

Comments: _____

_____

# READING AND RESOURCE LIST

## BOOKS

*Flip Chart Power: Secrets of the Masters,* by Bonnie E. Burn, Jossey-Bass/Pfeiffer, 1996.

*Getting to Yes: Negotiating Agreement Without Giving In,* by Roger Fisher, William Ury, and Bruce Patton (editor). Houghton Mifflin Co., 2nd edition, 1992.

*Great Meetings! How to Facilitate Like a Pro,* by Dee Kelsey, Pam Plumb, and Kippy Rudy (illustrator), Hanson Park Press, 1999.

*How to Lead Work Teams,* by Fran Rees, Jossey-Bass/Pfeiffer, 2001.

*Handbook of Organization Development in Schools and Colleges,* by Richard A. Schmuck and Philip J. Runkel, 4th edition, Waveland Press, 1994.

*101 Ways to Make Meetings Active: Surefire Ideas to Engage Your Group,* by Mel Silberman and Kathy Clark, Pfeiffer, 1999.

*People Skills,* Robert Bolton, Simon & Schuster, 1986.

*The Skilled Facilitator,* by Roger Schwarz, Jossey-Bass, 2002.

## VIDEO

*Meetings, Bloody Meetings: Making Meetings More Productive,* with John Cleese, Video Arts, 1993.

# WEB RESOURCE

www.grove.com: Process tools for meeting facilitators

# INDEX

## F

Facilitator: choosing, 38–39; responsibilities of, 14–15. *See also* Meetings, facilitation

Flip charts, 52

## G

Ground rules, 45–46, 53; for behavior, 55–56; establishing, 45; examples of, 46

## I

Ideas, sharing, 3

Information: capturing essential, 49–51; sharing, 3, 6

Invitees. *See* Participants

Issues, 4–5

## K

Key people, 6–7

## L

Language: clarifying, 55

## M

Meetings: criteria for effective, 7–10; length of, 28–31; preparation checklist for, 83; preparing for, 39–40; reasons for, 2–6; reasons to not hold, 6–7; roles and responsibilities in, 11–21; sample, evaluation, 85–87; worksheet for planning, 77–78

Meetings, facilitation: and capturing essential information, 49–51; and closing meeting, 56–58; common problems in, 55–56; and ensuring understanding of announcements and decisions, 54–55; and opening meeting, 45–49; overview, 41–42; and productive discussions, 51–56; and starting on time, 42–44. *See also* Facilitator

## O

Objective, identifying, 24–26

Open recording, 18–19

Open-ended questions, 51–52, 53

Opening, meeting, 45–49; activities, 46–47

## P

Participants: and deciding whom to invite, 31–33; ensuring understanding of announcements and decisions by, 54–55; notifying, 37; responsibilities of, 19–21

Participation: how to encourage, 53–54

Patience, 53

Perspectives, sharing, 3

Place, choosing, 34–35

Planning: and deciding whom to invite, 31–33; and factors about meeting place, 34–35; and factors about meeting time, 33–34; and identifying purpose and objective of meeting, 25–26; and length of meeting, 28–31; overview, 23–24; and preliminary list of agenda items, 27–28; and preparation checklist, 83; and preparing agenda and notifying participants, 36–38; process of, 24–25; as reason to hold meeting, 4; and seating arrangements, 35–36; worksheet for, 77–78

Presenter, responsibilities of, 16, 17

Problem, identification and resolution, 3–4

Purpose, identifying, 24–26

## R

Recorder: choosing, 25, 38–39; and open recording, 18–19; responsibilities of, 17–19; rotating, 18; seated among group, 50; standing in front of group, 50–51; and use of flip charts, 52